ROSA PARKS

"Tired of Giving In"

Anne Schraff

Series Consultant:
Dr. Russell L. Adams, Chairman
Department of
Afro-American Studies,
Howard University

Enslow Publishers, Inc.

40 Industrial Road	PO Box 38
Box 398	Aldershot
Berkeley Heights, NJ 07922	Hants GU12 6BP
USA	UK

http://www.enslow.com

"THE ONLY TIRED I WAS,
WAS TIRED OF GIVING IN."

—Rosa Parks

Library of Congress Cataloging-in-Publication Data

Schraff, Anne E.
    Rosa Parks : "tired of giving in" / Anne Schraff.
        p. cm. — (African-American biography library)
    Includes bibliographical references and index.
    ISBN 0-7660-2463-6 (hardcover)
    1. Parks, Rosa, 1913–   .—Juvenile literature. 2. African American
women—Alabama—Montgomery—Biography—Juvenile literature. 3. African
Americans—Alabama—Montgomery—Biography—Juvenile literature. 4. Civil rights
workers—Alabama—Montgomery—Biography—Juvenile literature. 5. African
Americans—Civil rights—Alabama—Montgomery—History—20th century—Juvenile
literature. 6. Segregation in transportation—Alabama—Montgomery—History—
20th century—Juvenile literature. 7. Montgomery (Ala.)—Race relations—Juvenile
literature. 8. Montgomery (Ala.)—Biography—Juvenile literature. I. Title. II. Series.
F334.M753P3866 2005
323'.092—dc22

2004015489

Printed in the United States of America

10 9 8 7 6 5 4 3 2 1

To Our Readers:
We have done our best to make sure all Internet Addresses in this book were active and appro-
priate when we went to press. However, the author and the publisher have no control over and
assume no liability for the material available on those Internet sites or on other Web sites they
may link to. Any comments or suggestions can be sent by e-mail to comments@enslow.com or
to the address on the back cover.

Every effort has been made to locate all copyright holders of material used in this book. If any
errors or omissions have occurred, corrections will be made in future editions of this book.

Illustration Credits: AP/Wide World, pp. 14, 17, 32, 35, 41, 55, 59, 62, 67, 69, 74, 75, 77, 86,
90–91, 95, 100, 103, 108, 110, 113; Library of Congress, pp. 7, 9, 18, 19, 24, 30, 45, 52;
Photographs and Prints Division, Schomburg Center for Research in Black Culture, The New
York Public Library, Astor, Lenox and Tilden Foundations, pp. 4, 80; Smithsonian Institution,
pp. 3, 26–27.

Cover Illustrations: Photographs and Prints Division, Schomberg Center for Research in
Black Culture, The New York Public Library, Astor, Lenox, and Tilden Foundations (portrait);
Smithsonian Institution (trolley car).

Contents

Chapter 1

The Right to Vote

Twenty-seven-year old Rosa Parks wanted to vote in the presidential election in 1940. Franklin D. Roosevelt was running for a third term as president. Parks liked Roosevelt, and she liked his wife even more. At a time when many Americans were divided by race, First Lady Eleanor Roosevelt believed in civil rights for all Americans, and she put her words into action.

Parks knew that registering to vote in Alabama was not easy for an African American in 1940. The white men who ran the government of Alabama and other states in the Deep South feared that African Americans might vote against them. They did not want to lose their power in the government. So the white

> "We were born and raised in America but we were treated as second-class citizens."[1]

politicians found many legal ways to avoid obeying the Fifteenth Amendment to the United States Constitution. This amendment had made it illegal to use race as a reason to deny any American citizen the right to vote.

Blacks who wanted to register to vote were threatened by their white employers. They were told they would lose their jobs if they tried to sign up. Voter registration sites were set up far from the neighborhoods where African Americans lived. It was hard for blacks to get to these places, especially because most of them did not own cars. Literacy tests were demanded, and African-American applicants were told they had failed even when they had the answers right. In addition, fees were charged for the privilege of voting. These were called poll taxes, and many poor blacks did not have the money to pay them.[2]

Segregation

At this time in the Deep South, segregation was the law. African Americans did not have the same rights and opportunities as white people did. They were forced to accept separate accommodations in schools, housing, entertainment, and just about every other aspect of their lives. The facilities for African Americans were separate— and they were inferior. In ways small and large, from water fountains and bathrooms to classrooms, African Americans were reminded of their second-class citizenship.

This water fountain was only for African Americans.

Rosa Parks was a strong-willed young woman, and despite all these obstacles she was determined to register to vote. In 1943, she studied her high-school government book to ready herself for the literacy test. Many of the questions would be about the Alabama constitution and what it meant.[3]

When Parks took the test, she knew the answers. She had surely passed the test. Over the next weeks, she waited for her voter registration card to come in the mail, but it never did. Sad and angry, Parks decided to try again. On a cold, rainy November day in 1943, she caught a bus to take her to the registration office. The bus was driven by a white man named James F. Blake. He set strict rules for his black passengers, and he made no exceptions. African Americans had to enter the bus in the front and pay their fare. Then they had to get off the bus and walk down to the side door. There they could get back on the bus and look for seats in the back. Segregation laws ordered all black passengers to sit at the back of the bus.

"They just told me, 'You didn't pass.' They didn't have to give you a reason."[4]

Rosa Parks boarded the bus at the front door and paid her fare. She refused to get off and reenter at the side door. She told Blake she saw no reason for it. The driver started pulling on her coat sleeve. "Get off my bus," he demanded.[5] Parks warned Blake not to strike her. Then, with her head held high, she stepped down off the bus.

For African Americans in the South, registering to vote was a challenge.

Parks determined to keep an eye out for Blake and stay off his bus in the future. That day she walked all the way to the registration office. She took the test and was told that she had failed.

The strategies whites used to keep blacks from voting worked very well. Even by 1960, in the neighboring state of Mississippi, only 5.3 percent of eligible black voters were ever registered.[6]

Rosa Parks made another attempt to register in 1944. Once again, she was told that she had failed the test.

In 1945 she was back. This time, she finished the test and then copied all twenty-one questions and her answers onto another sheet of paper. She knew she had all the right answers. If she was told again that she had failed to pass, she would have proof that the registrar was dishonest.

On this fourth try, Rosa Parks finally got her registration card in the mail. Only one obstacle remained—the poll tax. She managed to scrape together the $16.50, which was almost her whole week's salary as a seamstress. At last, for the first time in her life, the thirty-two-year-old seamstress would be able to vote. Parks had proved to herself that she must never give up fighting for her rights. And she had only begun to fight.

Chapter 2

Alabama Childhood

osa Louise McCauley was born February 4, 1913, in Tuskegee, Alabama. A small, underweight baby, she was the first child of Leona and James McCauley.

Leona Edwards, Rosa's mother, had been a teacher at several church-run schools in Pine Level, Alabama. She always treasured learning. Rosa later remembered her mother as a "woman of determination who believed in reading the Bible for guidance."[1] She prayed over her daughter every night, asking the Lord to protect and guide her.

Rosa's father, James McCauley, was a carpenter from Abbeville, Alabama, with thick, wavy hair. His grandmother was part Indian, and he was often mistaken for a Cherokee or Creek Indian. McCauley traveled all over

Alabama building houses. A strong, well-built man, he was a capable stonemason and carpenter.

The young couple had met when both were twenty-four years old. They were married at the Mount Zion African Methodist Episcopal (AME) Church in Pine Level on April 12, 1912. The newlyweds moved to Tuskegee, where they lived in a small frame house with a brick chimney. McCauley's construction work kept him constantly away from home, and his young wife was often left alone. When McCauley's younger brother, Robert, moved into the house, Leona had to cook and clean for him as well as care for baby Rosa. Rosa's mother was unhappy and frustrated.[2]

Rosa was baptized at age two in the AME Church. She often suffered from tonsillitis as a small child and spent many days in bed with a fever and sore throat. The doctor recommended a tonsillectomy, the removal of the infected tonsils, but the family was too poor to afford the operation.

When Leona McCauley was expecting her second child, the loneliness of her life became too much. Leona and James moved in with James's parents and large extended family. Four children had to share one bedroom. Making matters worse, the floors in the house were often dirty, and Leona, an excellent housekeeper, demanded cleanliness. Rosa's mother worked hard to bring the house up to her standards. Still, she did not get along with her husband's parents, causing unhappiness all around.

After spending less than a year with her in-laws, Leona McCauley packed up Rosa and all her meager possessions and went home to her parents' farm in Pine Level. Rosa's grandparents raised vegetables and chickens. James McCauley continued working around the state, traveling with his hammer and his saw and little else. Rosa did not see her father again until she was about two and a half years old, and then again when she was five. After that, she did not see him until she was grown and married.

Rosa's little brother, Sylvester, was born at their grandparents' farm. The family adjusted well to life with Grandfather Sylvester and Grandmother Rose. Rosa later described her grandmother as "strong willed . . . calm spirited and not easily excited."[3] Rosa's grandfather Sylvester Edwards had fair skin and looked like a white man. But he was filled with hostility to white people. He had been treated badly by whites, and he would never forget it.

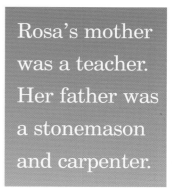

Rosa's mother was a teacher. Her father was a stonemason and carpenter.

At that time in Alabama, black people were required to show respect and deference to whites. For example, a black person was never to shake hands with a white person because that would imply that they were equals. Sometimes Edwards took advantage of his light skin, reaching out to shake the hands of white men and calling them by their first names. As an African American, he was

The Ku Klux Klan terrorized
African Americans throughout the South.

gambling with his life by doing this, but that did not stop him from playing this secret joke on whites.

Edwards's resentment of white people came from bitter personal experience. Born into slavery, Sylvester Edwards had been brutally treated on the plantation. As a boy, he was given no shoes and was often hungry because the slaves were not given enough to eat.[4]

Rosa learned many things from her grandfather. She credited him with teaching her about courage and the willingness to stand up against all odds for her beliefs.[5]

At the time of Rosa's childhood, the Ku Klux Klan (KKK) was very active in the Southern states. The Klan was a terrorist organization of white people who hated blacks. Klansmen rode on horses through the nights, hidden under frightening white robes and hoods to terrify African Americans. They beat or murdered those they considered to be troublemakers, and they burned African-Americans' homes and churches.

Rosa was about six years old when her grandparents told her to wear her clothes to bed so she could flee quickly in case the KKK came. To protect his family, Sylvester Edwards often slept in a rocking chair near the front door with a double-barreled shotgun across his knees. He said he probably could not stop the KKK if they broke into the house, but at least he would get "the first one that came in."[6] Little Rosa would sometimes curl up on the floor and sleep beside the rocker. "Whatever happened, I wanted to see it," she said. "I wanted to see him shoot that gun."[7]

The Value of Hard Work

Leona McCauley, Rosa's mother, was very impressed with the principles of hard work and thriftiness. She admired the work being done at the Tuskegee School in Tuskegee, Alabama, where African Americans were being educated in academic subjects like English and history, as well as being trained in carpentry and dressmaking. These were skills they could use to make a living.

The KKK sometimes paraded past the Edwards' house, but they never tried to get in.

Rosa's mother and grandparents were very religious, and Bible reading and prayers were a daily practice. "[My grandmother] would always read the Bible to me and my grandfather would pray," Rosa said later.[8]

To add to the family income, Rosa joined other local black children working for a wealthy white planter in Pine Level. Moses Hudson hired the children to pick and chop cotton. Rosa worked from sunup to sundown with the midday sun burning into her body. She would never forget how "the hot sun burned our feet whether or not we had our old work shoes on."[9] When the blisters on their feet became so large and painful that they could no longer walk, the children had to work on their knees, inching along the rows of cotton. A child whose blisters bled and stained the cotton would be whipped.

When Rosa was not picking cotton, she made money selling eggs and chickens. Still, there was also time for

Like this woman and little girl,
Rosa picked cotton as a child to earn money.

carefree joy in Rosa's childhood. Rosa took great pleasure in her role as big sister to Sylvester, who was two years and seven months younger than she was. Sylvester looked up to his older sister and followed her everywhere. Sister and brother explored the dense pine thickets and the creeks and ponds where they lived. Rosa liked to scoop crawfish from the many creeks so her mother could boil them with fresh corn. The family was poor, but there was always enough to eat. Fried ham with red-eye gravy, catfish fillets,

Black children were crowded into classrooms with little heat and few supplies.

The schools for white children in the South
were much better than the schools for black children.

fried rabbit, turnip greens, creamed peas, and pearl onions appeared on the table along with sweet-potato pie.

When Rosa was nine years old, the family could finally afford to have her tonsils removed, lifting the burden of frequent sick spells from the little girl's life. After she started school in Pine Level, she learned painful lessons about racism. White children would sometimes hurl rocks and insults at her and her brother as they walked to school. One day a white boy on roller skates tried to knock

Going to school, Rosa learned some painful lessons about racism.

Rosa off the sidewalk. Black children were taught not to respond to such abuse, but Rosa was a spirited child. She gave the boy a hard shove. When the boy's mother appeared and threatened her with jail for striking her son, Rosa calmly told the woman that her son had started the fight. Shocked by the child's boldness, the woman took her boy and hurried off. Rosa was lucky that the woman did not pursue the matter.

The white school in Pine Level was a clean brick building near a playground, but the school for black children was in poor shape. Sixty students crowded onto benches. There were no windows, desks, or books. Still, the teachers worked hard, and Rosa liked school. She loved reciting Mother Goose rhymes and reading stories. She enjoyed playing games with the other children.

Schooling for black children in Pine Level lasted only five months a year because most of the black families needed their children to work in the fields and raise money for family needs. Everyone was busy at planting time in the spring and harvest time in the fall. Schools for white children, on the other hand, were open for nine months.

Rosa always knew that white children were treated better than black children, and she later said that she had been "bothered by the fact that white children had privileges that I did not."[10]

When Rosa was eleven, she and her cousin Annie Mae went into a downtown store and asked for sodas. The clerk told the girls that black children could only have ice cream cones, which they must take outside. Sodas were served in glasses at the counter inside the store. African Americans were not allowed to sit at the counter. "We don't serve sodas to colored people," the clerk said.[11]

In spite of this, Rosa was taught by her mother and grandparents to be proud of herself and other African Americans and not to judge others as a group.[12] Whenever Rosa suffered a slight at the hands of a white person, she thought about instances when other whites had been kind. For instance, an elderly white woman in Pine Level often took Rosa bass fishing using crawfish tails for bait.

With her own strong love of learning, Rosa's mother was determined that her daughter receive a better education than she could get in Pine Level. So when Rosa was eleven years old, she had to leave her grandparents' farm for the big city of Montgomery, Alabama, and a whole new world.

Chapter 3

Education and Marriage

ard times were hitting Alabama in the early 1920s. The cotton crop on which so many poor farmers, black and white, depended was in trouble. The boll weevil, an insect that uses its long, sharp snout to pierce a hole in young cotton bolls, had arrived. The weevils lay eggs inside the cotton, and the eggs hatch into wormlike grubs that eat the cotton fiber and seeds. Cotton plantations were devastated by the boll weevils. For the wealthy plantation owners, there was a need to cut some of the luxuries out of their lives. But for the black farmers who had no money left over for extras, the destruction of their cotton meant hunger. Malnutrition spread through the Alabama Black Belt, the forty-five-thousand-mile strip of rolling country with rich black soil ideal for cotton. Fresh fruit, vegetables, and milk vanished from the diets of the poor. Now they lived on salt pork, hominy grits, and cornbread. It was not a good time for Rosa McCauley to be going to Montgomery to a private school that charged tuition.

Yet Rosa's mother and grandparents knew it was Rosa's only chance for a decent education. The money problem was solved when Rosa agreed to clean two classrooms daily in exchange for her tuition. In 1924, Rosa entered Montgomery Industrial School for girls. Called a progressive school, it taught practical skills, academics, and a philosophy that all students must strive for excellence. The greatest focus was on skills such as cooking, sewing, and housekeeping. The girls were being trained as future wives and mothers, and to work as maids, cooks, and housekeepers. These occupations were typical for most young African-American women of that time.

Montgomery Industrial School was located in the Centennial Hill section of the city, the center of black intellectual life in Montgomery. All public and private schools in Alabama were segregated by race, so while the teachers at the school were white, all the students were black.

Founded in 1866 by Miss Alice L. White, a white northern woman with a passion for educating blacks after the Civil War, Montgomery Industrial School had about 250 to 300 students. White was a strict disciplinarian, but she truly loved her students and tried to help them make the most of their lives. Rosa learned a great deal from Miss White, especially a sense of dignity and self-worth. White

Rosa Parks learned to sew in a class like this.

drilled it into the minds of all the girls, including Rosa, that they must never lower their sights in life because they were black.[1] This lesson remained with Rosa all her life.

Rosa was a good, quiet student. Even at home in Pine Level, she had few close friends and she was dutiful in doing all her chores. Just as she obeyed her mother and did what was expected of her without being reminded at home, she acted the same at Montgomery Industrial School. She always sat up straight at her desk and avoided any trouble. The students were offered dancing lessons, but Rosa's strict Baptist upbringing had convinced her that dancing was immoral, so she refused them.[2]

To eleven-year-old Rosa McCauley, the city of Montgomery, Alabama, was very large compared to Pine Level. For the first time in her life, Rosa heard people discussing segregation in a critical way. She had never liked the rigid system of dividing society between blacks and whites, with the blacks getting the worst of the bargain, but she had always accepted it as the way things were and would probably always be. Now her fellow students were talking about a group of blacks who had actually tried to change things twenty years earlier. It was exciting to hear about it. For the first time in Rosa's life, she considered that perhaps segregation was not going to be the system forever.

In 1900, in Montgomery, a group of black ministers had tried to change the way black riders were treated on the trolleys. Blacks were insulted and harassed, so the ministers asked all black riders to stay off the trolleys and walk instead for a few days. That way, the trolley company would see how much it needed the business of black riders. Then, perhaps, the black riders would be treated with more respect. The boycott started in August and continued for five weeks. The white-run trolley company ended segregation, allowing African Americans to sit anywhere they wanted on the trolleys. The boycott had been successful.

By the 1920s, segregation on the trolleys was back, and African-American riders were again discriminated against.

For Rosa, learning about the boycott provided exciting evidence that change was possible, and this stayed in her mind.

Rosa attended Montgomery Industrial School until 1928, when the school closed. Alice White had never been accepted by the white people of Montgomery. A white northern woman teaching equality to the local black population was unwelcome, to say the least. Education of black people was feared as a threat to the way things were. So there was always pressure to close the school. Finally, White, who had become old, blind, and frail, left town. She returned to Massachusetts, and her students were scattered to different institutions.

Fifteen-year-old Rosa McCauley attended ninth grade at a public school, Booker T. Washington Junior High. She finished the tenth and eleventh grades at the Laboratory School at Alabama State Teachers College. Rosa had dreams of becoming a teacher like her mother. But before Rosa could finish her senior year, she learned that her beloved Grandmother Rose was very ill. Nobody in the family told Rosa to quit school and return to Pine Level, but she did. Years later, Rosa explained her decision. "My grandmother was so generous and loving I felt it was time for me to give back to her."[3] So, when she was sixteen, Rosa took care of her grandmother and looked for a part-time job in Pine Level. She could not find work, so after her grandmother died, she returned to Montgomery. Finishing high school would have to wait, because she

Blacks and whites had to sit in separate sections of streetcars and city buses.

needed money. Rosa found a job at a textile factory making blue denim men's shirts. Then more bad news came from home. Rosa's mother was very ill. Leona McCauley suffered from severe migraine headaches and painfully swollen feet. Rosa returned to Pine Level to care for her mother.

> Rosa left school to help her family.

When her mother was feeling better, Rosa went back to Montgomery, her education again put aside so she could earn money. Rosa worked as a housekeeper, did some sewing with the skills she had learned from Miss White, and sold fruit at roadside stands. She joined the St. Paul AME Church in Montgomery.

As in Pine Level, Rosa's life revolved around the church. Between her work and her church, eighteen-year-old Rosa was very busy. She hated racism and discrimination but did not know much about the civil rights struggle. Before long, she would find herself plunging into the world of activism.

Rosa McCauley met twenty-eight-year-old Raymond Parks, a barber from Wedowee, a village in Alabama. Parks was in Montgomery working at the O. L. Campbell Barbershop, and he served as a caretaker in the AME Church. A mutual friend introduced the young couple. Raymond Parks's father was a carpenter who had been killed in a fall from a roof when Raymond was a baby. Parks's mother, Geri Culbertson Parks, had died when the boy was a teenager. Like Rosa McCauley, Raymond spent a lot of time caring for ailing relatives. From the moment that he saw her, Parks was interested in McCauley, but she was not attracted to him at first.[4]

After turning Parks down several times, McCauley finally agreed to go out for a ride in his shiny red car, which she admired. McCauley was impressed with Parks during that first date. As a person who had been taught to stand up for her rights, McCauley liked talking to other African Americans who had the same attitude. She liked the pride that Parks had.[5] McCauley had admired her tough-minded Grandfather Sylvester, who would not bow before whites, and Raymond Parks seemed to be "a good man, full of courage and inner strength."[6] She was also impressed by his intelligent conversation.[7] Although Parks had no formal education, his vast knowledge of books was striking.

Organizing for Civil Rights

In May 1909, a group of activists, both blacks and whites, formed an organization to work for civil rights. The National Association for the Advancement of Colored People (NAACP) has been a major force in the struggle for equality of African Americans. Raymond Parks was a founding member of the Montgomery chapter of the NAACP. Parks was well informed on current issues, and he read all the black newspapers and magazines.

The NAACP worked to help African Americans gain equal rights under the law.

◆ ◆ ◆ ◆ ◆

When McCauley first met Parks, he was deeply involved in one particular criminal case—the fate of a group of young black men known as the Scotts-boro Boys. Parks saw the predicament of the young men as a terrible injustice. McCauley later said, "It gnawed at him to see those innocent kids were framed."[8] Parks told McCauley he could not sleep at night until the nine young men were freed.

During the 1930s in the United States, the Great Depression was under way. Millions of people had no jobs and could not afford to buy food. Thousands lost their homes. Some unemployed men, both black and white, rode the trains, traveling from town to town in search of jobs. They waited for a slow-moving train, then jumped into open cars. They hopped off at the next town in the hope of finding work there.

On March 25, 1931, a group of young men, seven whites and nine blacks, were riding in a train car in

Scottsboro along with two white women. A fight broke out between the two groups of young men, and the blacks threw the whites off the train as it slowed down in Scottsboro. The white men reported the incident to the local sheriff. When the train arrived in the Scottsboro station, a sheriff's posse was waiting. The lawmen arrested the nine black men and the two white women. All were taken to county jail.

After this point, there was a disagreement over what happened. The nine blacks were accused of raping the white women. The youths denied it. The women were examined, and no evidence was found to indicate that such a crime had happened.[9] But word quickly spread through Scottsboro that nine black youths had raped two white women. An angry mob of white men surrounded the jail where the blacks were being held. Only the intervention of the sheriff, with state militia soldiers present, prevented the lynching of the youths that night.

The Scottsboro youths ranged in age from twelve to the mid-twenties. They were not from Alabama. One

Lynching

The idea of justice in the courts for African Americans accused of a crime was often just a dream in the American South in the 1930s. Being accused of a crime often led to lynching. In a lynching, a person is seized by a mob and put to death—often by hanging—without a trial. Between 1889 and 1940, there were about four thousand lynchings in the South, mostly of African Americans.

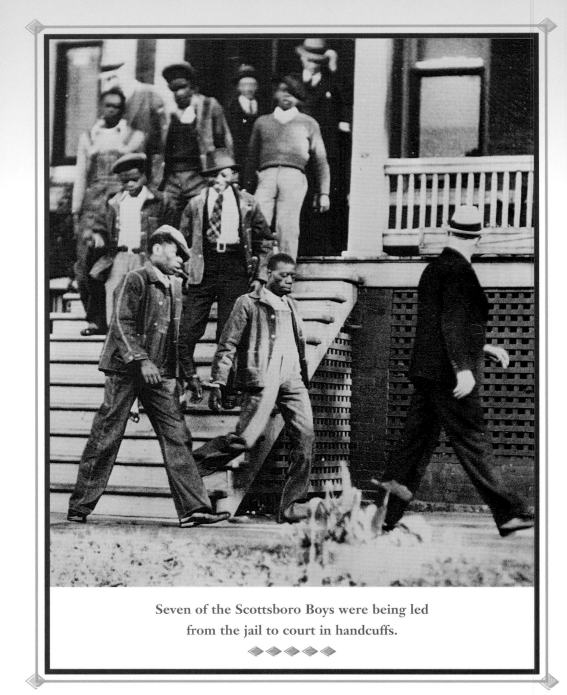

Seven of the Scottsboro Boys were being led
from the jail to court in handcuffs.

young man was almost blind, and another was disabled. None of them could read or write. They insisted they were innocent of anything but throwing the white men off the train.

The nine black youths were put on trial before an all-white jury. The trial lasted three days. All nine were convicted, and eight were sentenced to death. Only the life of the twelve-year-old was spared.

Raymond Parks and other civil rights leaders formed the National Committee to Defend the Scottsboro Boys. They spent hours trying to raise money for legal counsel to defend the condemned youths. These young men were facing death for a crime they did not commit. Parks took part in many meetings where strategy for freeing the youths was discussed. Rosa McCauley deeply admired his dedication. She watched him raising money and holding secret meetings. "He could have been beaten or killed for what he was doing," she said.[10] Parks would not let McCauley come to the meetings because he worried about the police breaking in. He was afraid she could not run fast enough to escape.

In the midst of his intensive work on the Scottsboro case, Raymond Parks proposed marriage to Rosa McCauley. She accepted because, as she would later say, he inspired her: "I list my husband, Raymond Parks, among the persons I admired most."[11] Rosa McCauley and Raymond Parks, whom Rosa always called "Parks," were married in 1932.

Chapter 1

The Strength to Work for Freedom

or Raymond Parks and other civil rights activists, their hard work paid off in the Scottsboro case. In 1932, the U.S. Supreme Court reversed the convictions. The reason was that the young men had not had an adequate defense. All nine had been defended during the trial by one volunteer lawyer. Alabama authorities hurried to arrange another trial. They were confident they would get another conviction and new death sentences.

Rosa and Raymond Parks, after being married in Rosa's mother's home, had no money for a honeymoon. They moved into a rooming house on South Jackson Street in Montgomery. There, Raymond Parks continued his work in behalf of the Scottsboro Nine. Meetings to plot strategy were held in the newlywed couple's small apartment. Raymond Parks and others sat around a small table to discuss raising enough money for good lawyers for the young men.

"The table was covered with guns," Rosa Parks later said.[1] During the meetings, she sat on the back porch, her face buried in her lap in sadness. She later said she was thinking about how sad it was that black men could not meet "without fear of bodily injury or death."[2]

In 1933, the Scottsboro Nine were retried even though one of the women who had accused them now admitted

Protesters marched to the White House in 1933 to ask President Roosevelt to help free the Scottsboro Boys.

that nothing had happened. Another white jury convicted the nine men, and the death penalty was again imposed. In April 1936, the Supreme Court overturned this verdict as well because no blacks had been permitted to serve on the jury.

By 1937, a compromise was reached regarding the case. The four youngest defendants were set free. The others would be paroled after a year. In spite of this, the last of the Scottsboro Nine did not gain his freedom until 1950, nineteen years after the alleged incident took place.

The Scottsboro case turned the quiet, almost passive Rosa Parks into a civil rights activist. As the young wife of Raymond Parks, she worked with him in civil rights matters. With his support she returned to high school, and in 1933 she earned her high school diploma. At the time, only seven out of every one hundred black people in Montgomery was a high school graduate.

The 1930s were especially hard economic years for black Americans. Excluded from the better jobs and with little or no savings, African Americans struggled. Rosa Parks became a nurse's assistant at St. Margaret's Hospital, and she sewed clothing for white clients in her free time to supplement her husband's salary as a barber.

In 1941, Rosa Parks got a job as a secretary at Maxwell Field Flight School and Air War College. Established by the Wright Brothers, who had successfully built and flown the first powered airplane, Maxwell Field school was on federal land. It was an eye-opening experience for Parks. Federal facilities were integrated. On the military base, for the first time in her life, Parks saw whites and blacks being treated equally. It was like stepping into a suddenly liberated world for the young black woman.

On the bus on the base, she could sit in any seat she wanted, but the moment she left Maxwell Field, she was hurled back into segregated Montgomery, taking her place with other blacks in the back of the city bus.

Rosa's younger brother, Sylvester McCauley, was drafted into the army to fight in World War II. The U.S. military was segregated, so McCauley would be serving in an all-black unit—the 1318th Medical detachment of the Engineering Services Regiment. He would be one of more than a million young African Americans serving in World War II, half of them sent to European battle zones. They were primarily assigned to noncombat status in support of white troops, but they were exposed to as much peril and suffered many casualties. Sometimes black and white troops fought side

African-American Soldiers

African Americans have answered the call to serve their country since the beginning of the United States. Five thousand fought in the American Revolution in the Continental Army. About 200,000 joined the Union army in the Civil War. In World War I, there were 367,000 African-American soldiers, and in World War II, more than one million.

by side under fire, as in the December 1944 bloody but decisive Battle of the Bulge near the French and Belgian border.

Seeing her brother in a military uniform impressed on Rosa Parks's mind how, in wartime, the black man was expected to do his duty just as the white man was. Why then in peacetime did he not deserve equal treatment?

Raymond Parks was growing annoyed at the slow pace of action on civil rights matters from the NAACP, so he quit the organization. At the same time, Rosa Parks joined the NAACP, with no argument from her husband. She had read an article in *Look* magazine about the NAACP director, Walter White. He was a bold African-American champion of civil rights. Rosa Parks was impressed by the plans White was proposing, and she saw great promise in the organization as a vehicle for the advancement of black rights.

White liked to tell a story about the time he accidentally stepped on a black man's foot in Harlem. The fair skinned, blue-eyed White looked white, and the black man saw him as just another white man with no respect for blacks. Then the offended black man realized he was talking to Walter White of the NAACP, and he apologized for taking offense.

The local director of the Montgomery NAACP was Edgar Daniel Nixon, or E. D. Nixon, as he was always called. A very tough-minded man, he reminded Rosa

Parks of her own grandfather. Nixon promoted nonviolent action, though he often carried a gun just in case. Since the Montgomery NAACP did not have enough money to rent an office, Nixon worked out of his home, and Parks volunteered her services as his secretary. She wrote letters, set up meetings, arranged speakers, and ran the office

> Rosa Parks joined the NAACP to help work for civil rights.

for Nixon. Her office skills, which had been honed working at Maxwell Field school, were outstanding.

Sometimes Rosa Parks took black children on field trips. On one trip, they visited the traveling Freedom Train. The train held an exhibit of documents important in American history, such as the Declaration of Independence and the Constitution. The train went on tour throughout the United States in the 1940s so young people could better understand their country. When white teachers showed up with their students and expressed annoyance at seeing the Freedom Train filled with Rosa Parks and her black children, she calmly ignored their displeasure.

Among the speakers who came to Montgomery to help in the voter registration drive was an outspoken Harlem lawyer, Arthur A. Madison. An Alabama native, he was fearless in his demands for African-American equality at the voting booth. The Montgomery police arrested him on a voting violation, and when he was freed, the NAACP did not do much to help him. He was seen as too much of a rabble-rouser. Rosa Parks was unhappy about this lack of support.

In 1945, the soldiers began returning home, including Sylvester McCauley. He had an excellent war record in both Europe and the Pacific. Married just before going into the army, he was now the father of a boy, Sylvester Jr.

McCauley was a medic in the army, and at the Battle of Normandy he helped carry hundreds of his wounded comrades to safety under enemy fire. Then he went to the Pacific, where he was also a stretcher-bearer during battle. He had been in the thick of the fighting, risking his life for his country. He expected that when he returned home, his white neighbors would respect him more. McCauley was in for a shock. Not only were the returning black veterans not treated well, but the white population at home was fearful that the black veterans would now demand equal rights. So the black veterans were often the target of harassment.

Even war prisoners had more rights. When German war prisoners were sent to work in the Mississippi fields, they would be taken to eat at local diners. There, they could walk in the front door and sit at the best tables. Yet the African-American soldiers guarding the German prisoners had to enter by the back door and eat their meals standing outside.

African-American soldiers fought valiantly in World War II, yet
they were discriminated against when they came home from the war.

Brutal assaults on the returning African-American veterans became frequent. "My very stomach turned over when I learned that Negro soldiers just back from overseas were being dumped out of army trucks and beaten," President Harry Truman said in 1945.[3]

One of the most horrifying examples of this behavior involved Sergeant Isaac Woodward, who was on his first furlough after fifteen months in the South Pacific. He boarded an interstate bus in Georgia, and was seen by the white driver as arrogant. Police were called onto the bus, and Woodward, who never drank any liquor, was arrested for public intoxication. The police then beat him with their blackjacks and nightsticks. The beating was so severe that Woodward's ribs were smashed and the corneas in both eyes were permanently damaged, leaving him blind for life.

Sylvester McCauley was also accused of being "uppity," a term the whites used to describe a black person who did not defer to them. McCauley was spat upon by some whites when he returned to Montgomery. His efforts to find a job were fruitless. McCauley learned the hard way that nothing had changed in spite of his service to his country. So he packed his wife, Daisy, and their two children into the car and got on Highway 61 going north. He was heading for Detroit, Michigan, and would never return to Montgomery. He hoped that life in the North would be better for African Americans.

McCauley got a job as a janitor at the Chrysler factory in Detroit, and he was immediately pleased with the new environment. Rosa Parks missed her brother, so she left Montgomery for the first time in her life to visit him for two weeks. When she got to Detroit, Parks was amazed by the integration of the races. She knew Detroit was not a segregated city, but to actually see the races mixing together was a revelation to her. She was experiencing the freedom of an integrated society for the first time, but, unlike her brother, she would not stay in Detroit.

For all the frustrations of Montgomery and segregation, Rosa Parks was homesick. She missed small things like Merritt's Beaten Biscuits and Buffalo Rock Ginger Ale, WCOV-AM radio, and gospel Sundays at St. Paul's AME Church. She missed the soul-food lunches at Ben Moore Hotel and collard greens at the local markets. But there was also another reason why Rosa Parks would not consider moving to Detroit. Parks heard about the race riots that had ravaged Detroit in 1943. A white mob had attacked an apartment house in the black area, and the violence grew until thirty-four blacks and nine whites were dead. Thousands were injured, and blocks of homes were burned down. Parks had seen a lot of bad things happen in Montgomery, but nothing on so frightening a scale. She wanted no part of living in Detroit.

> Rosa's brother moved north in search of a better life.

When Rosa Parks returned to Montgomery, her

contribution to the NAACP increased. Working with clients in the NAACP office, Parks developed a deep knowledge of their problems. Her conversation skills grew. She was now a valuable NAACP activist whose gifts were recognized. She was invited to speak to a large audience at the October 1948 NAACP state convention in Mobile, Alabama. Though Parks had never spoken before a large group, she conquered her fear and did a fine job talking about the problems of black people in Montgomery. These were the issues she dealt with on a daily basis. After making this speech, Parks gained more confidence in herself and her abilities.

Rosa Parks was employed at Crittenden's Tailor Shop in Montgomery, where she altered men's suits and handsewn dresses. She was a skilled seamstress. Life was comfortable for Rosa and Raymond Parks, and the work she did for the NAACP added greatly to her sense of satisfaction.

The Parks were childless, and the nieces and nephews were far away in Detroit, so Rosa Parks fulfilled her desire to help children by working in the NAACP youth group. She served as an adviser and friend to many boys and girls. As E. D. Nixon commented later, "Kids just love Mrs. Parks to death. They had a special bond, an understanding that was very rare indeed, full of hugs and all that."[4] Parks also taught Sunday school at St. Paul's AME Church.

Parks had to put aside her work at the NAACP when her mother's health worsened. Her mother needed Rosa's care.

By 1952, Leona McCauley was better, and Parks was able to resume volunteering for the NAACP. In 1954, the United States Supreme Court handed down a landmark decision in *Brown* v. *Board of Education of Topeka, Kansas*, which said that segregated schools were unconstitutional. The schools were supposedly "separate but equal," but the schools for African-American children were far from equal.

In 1954, the Supreme Court declared that school segregation was unconstitutional.

The Court ruled that forcing black children to attend a different school from whites gave the black children the idea that something was wrong with them.

It was about this time that Rosa Parks met a white couple who were to play a major role in her life. Clifford and Virginia Durr were civil libertarians and champions of the downtrodden. Virginia Durr had been raised in Alabama in a wealthy family. When she went to college, she became aware of the injustice of segregation. She decided she would devote her life to helping victims of discrimination.

Clifford Durr was a lawyer who shared his wife's crusading spirit. Since the Durrs devoted most of their time to working, without fees, for poor people, they were soon struggling financially themselves. They moved with their three children to Montgomery, Alabama, to live with Clifford Durr's mother. Clifford Durr started the Durr Law Firm to handle local civil rights cases. The couple aroused the suspicion and animosity of the Montgomery white community, which labeled the Durrs Communists. E. D. Nixon introduced Rosa Parks, his secretary, to the Durrs, and a friendship grew. Virginia Durr hired Parks to sew clothing for the Durr daughters. Virginia Durr later recalled that Parks never charged enough money for her work, so Durr would insist on paying more. Virginia Durr called Rosa Parks "one of the greatest" people she had ever met and a real "southern lady."[5] She became one of Rosa Parks's closest friends.

Financial hardship was becoming part of Rosa and Raymond Parks's lives. Raymond was missing a lot of work because of illness. Rosa was again spending a great deal of time with her sick mother and holding down several part-time jobs to make ends meet.

Rosa Parks and the Durrs began to discuss the issue of mistreatment of black riders on the Montgomery bus lines. It was not enough that blacks had to sit in the back of the buses, but when the buses were crowded they were expected to yield even those rear seats to white riders. Also, white bus drivers often ridiculed and harassed black riders. They were routinely addressed in demeaning ways. Grown black men were called "boy," and black grand-mothers were called "girl."

African Americans made up 75 percent of the ridership of the Montgomery buses. They were generally too poor to own cars, while most of the Montgomery whites drove to their destinations in their own cars. Since the black riders were the economic backbone of the bus system, it seemed they ought to be treated with respect.

Virginia Durr knew how dedicated Rosa Parks was to advancing equality, but Parks had no formal training in how to bring about change. There was a work-shop in Monteagle, Tennessee, in the Appalachian Mountains, which trained blacks and whites together in the skills of organizing and mobilizing civil rights

> White bus drivers were often nasty to black riders.

activists. The Highlander Folk School was founded by Myles and Zilphia Horton in 1932. It was funded by the Durrs and like-minded whites. A teacher and community activist, Horton lived by the motto that "people are not powerless. With guidance, they can solve their own problems."[6] Mrs. Durr believed that Parks would benefit greatly from attending the Highlander Folk School, so she arranged a two-week scholarship.

Rosa Parks took a leave of absence from her job at Montgomery Fair Department Store, the largest retail store in the city, where she now worked as a seamstress. She set off to learn new strategies for fighting racism. Raymond Parks was not pleased with his wife's decision to attend the workshop because he feared the school promoted revolution. Backers of the Highlander Folk School over the years had included Eleanor Roosevelt, wife of President Franklin Roosevelt, and Dr. Martin Luther King, Jr., along with many other Americans interested in civil liberties for all people.

When the forty-two-year-old Parks first arrived at Highlander, she felt out of place. She was not at ease when the discussions began around the tables. The mostly white participants called one another "brother," and "sister," and there was a casual, folksy atmosphere that the prim, reserved Parks was not accustomed to. But then Parks began telling her own stories about abuses she had learned about and witnessed as an NAACP counselor.

Everybody listened attentively, and she grew more comfortable. She talked about the ill treatment her war veteran brother received when he came home, and she shared horror stories from the field work she had done from E. D. Nixon's office.

It turned out that Rosa Parks had a great deal to offer these white liberal activists, and they appreciated her first-hand accounts of situations they had only read about. Seeing the concern and respect in their eyes gave Parks courage, and soon she felt at home at Highlander.

Rosa Parks had an experience at Highlander Folk School that was new to her. For the first time in her life, she was eating food cooked and served by other people. Her breakfast arrived on a tray. Somebody else fried her eggs and bacon and made her bed. Somebody else brewed her coffee. For Parks, who had always done the serving, it was a strange and wonderful feeling to be pampered.

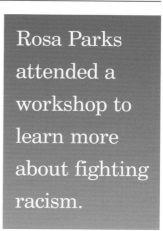

Rosa Parks attended a workshop to learn more about fighting racism.

Attending Highlander Folk School was a healthy, liberating experience for Rosa Parks. Whites and blacks here shared the same ideals. In this mountain haven, they were all working for the same goal—a color-blind society. Parks began to believe that such a world was possible, and she resolved to work even harder for that vision. "I gained the strength to persevere in my work for freedom," Parks later said.[7]

Chapter 5

The Arrest

W hen Rosa Parks returned to her job at Montgomery Fair Department Store, she felt let down. At Highlander, in the beautiful Appalachian Mountains, she had experienced equality and hope, but now she was back in the real world. She worked in a sweltering room without air conditioning, spending long hours sewing, and then rode home in a segregated bus.

On August 14, 1955, Parks attended an NAACP meeting at the Metropolitan United Methodist Church. There she met the Reverend Martin Luther King, Jr., for the first time. Only about thirty people had showed up to hear the young black minister discuss the implications of the Supreme Court decision desegregating schools. Parks was immediately impressed with King. "Dr. King was a true leader," she said later. "I never sensed fear in him."[1]

Also in August, a particularly horrible crime shocked Rosa Parks and all of America. Fourteen-year-old Emmett

THE ARREST

Till was visiting his uncle in Money, Mississippi. Emmett was from Chicago, and he was not used to the Deep South. When his friends dared him, he allegedly said, "Bye, baby" and whistled at a white clerk in a country store. Emmett had no idea that this was considered a serious offense. The woman told her husband, and a group of angry white men went in search of the boy. They kidnapped him, and took him into the woods. Later, his mangled body was found in the Tallahatchee River. Shockwaves raced through the black community when a photograph of the dead boy's face was shown in *Jet* magazine. His face was so bruised and distorted that he was barely recognizable as a person. Emmett's mother had wanted the whole world to see what had been done to her child after he was accused of being sassy to a white woman.

What happened next was even worse. The two white men arrested for the crime were put on trial. The trial lasted five days, and eyewitnesses identified the men positively. The all-white jury deliberated for one hour before finding the suspects not guilty and setting them free. Rosa Parks and many others wept over what happened. Now Parks was more determined than ever to do something about the racial injustice around her.

Still, during the summer of 1955, Parks went about her life as usual, not making any major changes. She worked

In the summer of 1955, a horrible crime shocked the nation.

After the brutal, senseless murder of
fourteen-year-old Emmett Till, Rosa Parks was more
determined than ever to fight against racism.

for the NAACP, and she worked to earn a living. Then, on a cold, rainy day, December 1, 1955, Parks left her job as usual and planned to go home. It was 5 P.M. when she walked to Court Square to wait for the bus.

> Parks and many others wept over what happened.

Rosa Park's body ached from the long hours she had spent at her work bench, and her feet were swollen and painful. She suffered from bursitis, which is pain and swelling near the joints. When she reached the bus stop, she found a large crowd there. That meant that when the bus came, many would get on ahead of her and she might have to make the trip home standing, clutching a strap. She decided to wait until the crowd thinned out and then try to board another bus.

Parks crossed the street to a store, hoping to buy a heating pad to relieve her pains. When she priced the heating pads, she found she could not afford one, so she bought a few small Christmas gifts instead. She returned to the bus stop carrying her shopping bag. When the bus came, she dropped her dime into the slot and started down the aisle without even looking at the bus driver. If she had looked at him, she would have recognized James Blake, the bus driver who had harassed her many years before, the driver whose bus she had avoided since that time.

On all Montgomery buses, the front seats were assigned to white passengers. The rear ten seats were allotted to black riders. The middle sixteen seats could be occupied by white or black passengers. It was up to the driver of each bus.

Rosa Parks found a seat near the back, in the middle section. She sat down next to a black man. Across the aisle sat two black women. Parks settled into the seat, glad to be off her feet, and she thought about home. At the next stop, more white people got on the bus. Very quickly, all the white seats filled up. One white man was left standing in the aisle.

The bus driver turned around, and his gaze locked on Rosa Parks. Their stares met, and Parks recognized James Blake. He came down the aisle and looked at the four black passengers seated toward the rear. The rule was that white passengers were not to be left standing. Blacks had to yield their seats, even in the black section. No white person was expected to sit in a row where black passengers were already seated, so all four black riders were supposed to get up and turn the row into a "white row."

"Y'all make it light on yourselves and let me have those seats," Blake said to the four black riders.[2] None of them moved. Blake repeated his demand, and, quietly, the two black women got up and stood, moving farther back. The black man beside Parks was sitting near the window. When he started to stand, Parks swung her legs over to let him get out. Then she moved to the window seat he had just vacated and began looking out the window.

> The bus driver's gaze locked on Rosa Parks.

Today, this bus is famous. It was on this bus that driver James Blake ordered Rosa Parks to stand up and give her seat to a white man.

Blake drew closer and said, "Look woman, I told you I wanted that seat. Are you going to stand up?" Parks replied softly, "No, I'm not."[3]

"Well, if you don't stand up, I'm going to call the police and have you arrested," Blake warned.

"You may do that," Rosa Parks quietly said.[4]

Blake called his supervisor and waited. As the bus sat there, the passengers, both black and white, grew increasingly nervous. They realized a serious confrontation was approaching, and they filed off the bus and looked for another way to get home.

Soon, two Montgomery police officers arrived on the scene, F. B. Day and D. W. Mixon. Parks sat silently watching as Blake explained the situation to the officers. Officer Day came down the aisle and asked Parks why she refused to stand when she was asked to do so by the driver.

"Why do you all push us around?" Parks asked.

"I do not know," said the officer, "but the law is the law and you're under arrest."[5] Later, Parks explained why she was willing to risk arrest that day. "Because I had endured that treatment so long," she said.[6] She had reached the end of her patience.

Officer Day picked up Parks's purse, and Officer Mixon took her shopping bag. They took Parks to their squad car. Once more Day asked Parks why she refused to stand and move when the driver spoke to her. But this time Rosa Parks did not answer him. She was very calm, but later she described that arrest as "one of the worst days of my life." She further said that only her faith in God kept her strong and composed.[8]

> "I did not get on the bus to get arrested; I got on the bus to go home."[7]

Parks was taken to the Montgomery City Hall to be processed. She was very thirsty by this time, and she longed for a drink of water. She noticed a water fountain in the room where they had taken her, and she asked if she might take a drink. Officer Day said yes, but Officer Mixon said the fountain was for whites only. He could not break the rules by letting a black woman drink from it.

Parks filled out all the required forms and asked to call

her husband. Raymond Parks was expecting her home at the usual time, and she knew he would be worried. The request was refused. Parks was taken from city hall in the squad car directly to city jail on North Ripley Street. There she was fingerprinted and mug shots were taken of her. Parks's handbag and shopping bag were taken into police custody. She was treated like a criminal.

Parks was led up a flight of stairs to the cells. The corridor reeked of foul smells. Rosa Parks was a diligent housekeeper, and her home always smelled clean. Here, it smelled like dirty toilets. Parks was put into a cell by herself on the second floor. The iron-barred door was closed. Later, Parks recalled thinking, "I felt as if the world had forgotten me. But I felt [God's] presence with me in the jail cell."[9] The guard returned then and asked Parks whether she would prefer to be in a larger cell with two other prisoners, or to be alone. Parks chose the larger cell and the company of the other women. She repeated her request to make a phone call to her husband. By now he would be very concerned that something had happened to her. But the guard refused her request and left her in the cell with the other women.

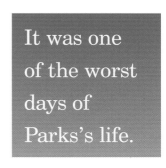

It was one of the worst days of Parks's life.

When Parks mentioned being thirsty, one of the women filled a tin cup with water and brought it to her. Then the woman told her own sad story. She had an abusive boyfriend, and to defend herself she had wielded a hatchet to force him to back off. The boyfriend had reported her to the police, and she was arrested. The poor woman was distraught because her family did not even know she was in jail. She did not have the money to bail herself out, and the guards would not let her call her brother to come get her. In the hopes that Rosa Parks might get out of jail sooner than she would, the woman scribbled her brother's phone number on a piece of paper and gave it to Parks, pleading with her to do what she could.

After another hour passed, Rosa Parks was finally allowed to make a phone call. When she called home, her mother answered. "I'm in jail," Parks said in a calm voice. "See if Parks will come down here and get me out."[10] Raymond Parks grabbed the phone when he realized his wife was on the line. He wanted to know if she was all right. Rosa assured him that she had not been abused. Raymond said he would get down to the jail in a few minutes. But that was easier said than done. The family did not own a car. It would take time to get a friend to drive down to the jail.

Word of Rosa Parks's arrest had in fact spread through the black community. Some people on the bus recognized her and saw her being arrested. Somebody telephoned E. D. Nixon's house, where his wife, Arlet, took the call. Arlet Nixon said to her husband, "You won't believe it. The police got Rosa. She's in jail."[11] E. D. Nixon called

The sheriff's department took a mug shot of Rosa Parks.

> Word of Rosa Parks's arrest spread through the black community.

the jail, but the police would give him no information.[12] It was routine that black callers were refused details of an arrest. All callers had to identify themselves, and if the police knew the person to be African American, no details of an arrest were given. Nixon contacted Clifford Durr, who called immediately. Since he was white, he was told that Rosa Parks had been arrested for violating the city's segregation ordinance and that her bail was set at $100.

Durr and Nixon headed down to city jail to pay the bail. At the same time, Raymond Parks had secured a ride and was also arriving at the jail. Durr and Nixon were surprised by how serene Rosa Parks looked as she came walking from the jail. Raymond Parks gave his wife a huge bear hug when he saw her.

At this point, the arrest of Rosa Parks was a minor incident, just another reminder of the humiliating and unfair bus system in Montgomery. But it soon became something much more. The night Rosa Parks came home from jail, E. D. Nixon and Clifford Durr were talking about making the arrest a test case of the constitutionality of segregation on the buses.

Rosa Parks, her husband, Nixon, and Durr talked for a long time about the possibility of using the arrest in the courts to test segregation. They also discussed boycotting the bus system in Montgomery to protest the arrest of

Parks. "We can break the buses," Nixon said.[13] By that he meant that since the majority of bus riders were black, if they boycotted the system, the bus company would go broke.

Montgomery was in the midst of a cold winter, with weather below freezing. Arlet Nixon doubted that black riders would go along with a boycott that required them to walk in the cold. E. D. Nixon insisted that the black people of Montgomery were disgusted enough by segregation on the buses that they would go along with the boycott no matter what the sacrifices were.

Raymond Parks did not like the idea of making his wife's arrest a major cause. He did not want her to be exposed to all the publicity and danger. If she became the focus of a major attempt to overturn bus segregation, he feared, she might become a target of white rage. "Rosa," he kept warning her, "the white folks will kill you."[14] He was not just being dramatic. He had deep, well-founded fears that as the struggle became more intense over the coming weeks and months, Rosa would be in real danger.

Rosa Parks did not take her decision lightly. She had serious concerns too. Her frail mother lived with her, and Rosa did not want her mother to be hurt. Raymond was not earning much money as a barber, and so Rosa was the

> Would the African-American community unite in boycotting city buses?

E. D. Nixon, center, head of the Montgomery NAACP,
and attorney Fred Gray, right, encouraged Parks
to go forward with a lawsuit.

main breadwinner for her mother and her husband. If the white community turned against her, putting pressure on her employer, she might be fired. Then what would happen? Almost all the employers in Montgomery were white. Parks worried that she would not be able to earn a living anymore in Montgomery. The NAACP was struggling financially and did not have the money to support the Parks family.

In the end, Parks decided she must overcome her fears and be willing to risk everything to advance the cause of freedom and justice. She would take on the Montgomery bus system. She told Nixon she would allow her case to be used to challenge the constitutionality of bus segregation. The legal costs of mounting the court case would be borne by the NAACP.

E. D. Nixon was jubilant at Parks's decision. He saw her as the perfect subject for a test case, a sweet, soft-spoken woman of flawless reputation who had worked hard all her life and never made any trouble. She was deeply religious and a lifelong member of the community. Angry whites often insisted that the local black people were perfectly content the way things were and that the only ones trying to change the system were "outside agitators" who probably were Communists. They could not pin these labels on Rosa Parks. She was a

> Parks decided that she was ready to risk everything to fight injustice.

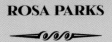
likable woman who just wanted to sit in her assigned seat on the bus without being harassed. One young black woman declared jubilantly, "She's so sweet. They've messed with the wrong one now!"[15] Many people repeated the story that Rosa Parks had stayed in her seat that day because she was simply too tired. "The only tired I was, was tired of giving in," Rosa Parks explained.[16]

Chapter 6

"The Miracle of Montgomery"

W hen Rosa Parks was released from jail, she kept her promise to her cellmate. She called the young woman's brother and told him of her plight. He quickly got his sister out of jail. Then, although the court case that would challenge the bus segregation ordinance was coming, Parks went back to her normal routine. On December 2, 1955, she reported to work as usual at the Montgomery Fair Department Store. Meanwhile, the black ministers of Montgomery were meeting with E. D. Nixon to plan a boycott of the bus system. Nixon believed the only African Americans in the city with enough influence to get the boycott moving were the ministers.

Nixon contacted the Reverend Ralph Abernathy, the twenty-nine-year-old pastor of the largest black Baptist church in Montgomery, the First Baptist Church.

Abernathy had the reputation of giving courageous civil rights sermons. He was fearless in his challenges to segregation.[1] Abernathy immediately embraced the boycott idea and scheduled a meeting with the city's other African-American ministers at Dexter Avenue Baptist Church. The pastor of that church was another dynamic young preacher, the Reverend Martin Luther King, Jr. After King joined the movement, the two men telephoned the other ministers.[2] King called all the Baptist ministers, and Abernathy phoned the Methodists. The one-day bus boycott was scheduled for Monday, December 5, 1955.

To get the word out that no African-American adult or child should ride the buses on Monday, all the preachers spoke of it in their Sunday sermons. Flyers were distributed throughout the African-American neighborhoods. Seven thousand leaflets were printed and distributed by women and young volunteers.

Early Monday morning, Rosa and Raymond Parks watched from their window to see if the bus boycott had worked. Rosa Parks prayed for its success, but she, along with the ministers, feared that it might fizzle out as weary blacks decided they could not manage long walks to work. When the first bus appeared, the Cleveland Avenue bus, the Parkses were thrilled to see that it was almost empty.

The African Americans of Montgomery had heeded the call of their ministers. There was a taxicab army of black drivers charging their passengers a reduced rate

The Reverend Martin Luther King, Jr., here at the
pulpit of Holt Street Baptist Church, led the bus boycott.

> At first, the boycott was planned as a one-day protest.

of ten cents a ride, the same fare as the buses.[3] Many African Americans simply walked, trudging through the city, carrying their tool boxes. African-American housewives walked with bags of laundry, and children ran after the empty buses, shouting. Everybody walked, took a cab, begged rides from friends, carpooled, or just postponed their errands.

The white leadership of Montgomery was outraged by the bus boycott. In spite of her spotless record as a peaceful, deeply Christian woman, Rosa Parks was branded by the powerful whites in the city as a Communist trouble-maker.[4]

On the same morning that the empty buses were rolling, Rosa Parks went to court on the charge of violating the bus segregation law. A large black crowd thronged around the Montgomery City Hall as Rosa and Raymond Parks walked in. Rosa Parks wore a long-sleeved black dress with white collar and cuffs, a black velvet hat, and a dark gray coat. As she entered the Recorders Court for her trial, she looked like a dignified middle-aged lady.

The courtroom was segregated, with whites in front and blacks in the back, and every seat was filled. The main witness was bus driver James Blake. He described exactly what had happened. Rosa Parks did not dispute his version of the incident. There was no doubt that Parks had refused to get up and yield her seat to the white man.

Parks, accompanied by E. D. Nixon, arrived at the courthouse.

Parks did not testify, but she pleaded not guilty. The trial lasted five minutes, and the verdict surprised no one. Rosa Parks was found guilty of violating the bus ordinance and fined $10 as well as $4 in court costs. She was now a convicted criminal. Although the black crowd outside groaned when they heard the verdict, E. D. Nixon and the other activists had gotten just what they needed. With a guilty verdict, they could now appeal to a higher court, eventually taking the case to federal courts including the Supreme Court. There they hoped bus segregation would go the way of school segregation and be declared unconstitutional.

A mass meeting was called for that evening to announce the formation of the Montgomery Improvement Association (MIA). Martin Luther King, Jr., was appointed leader. The demands of the MIA were not extreme. They asked for drivers to show courtesy to black passengers just as they did to white passengers. They demanded a stop to humiliating rudeness against black riders. They asked that seating on the bus be on a first-come, first-served basis, and if all the white seats were filled, black passengers would not be asked to give up their seats. Also, the MIA asked for black bus drivers on the heavily black routes. Since the one-day boycott had been so successful, the MIA decided to continue the boycott until their demands were met.

The white leaders of Montgomery were outraged— and branded Parks a troublemaker.

King addressed the mass meeting with Rosa Parks sitting quietly behind him. He called Parks a woman of "integrity," "character," and "Christian commitment."[5] King was delighted with the great support the black community had given the bus boycott. He called it "the miracle of Montgomery."[6] King described Parks's arrest as "the precipitating factor," of the protest and hailed all the black people "willing to substitute tired feet for tired souls."[7]

On January 7, 1956, Rosa Parks was dismissed from her job at Montgomery Fair Department Store. They told her they were closing their tailor shop and she was no longer needed. She received two weeks pay and some bonus money. Although there was suspicion that her dismissal had something to do with her new fame as the focus of the boycott, Parks herself disputed this. She insisted that she had no reason to believe her stand had anything to do with the loss of her job.[8] It was a sign of her scrupulous honesty that Parks would be fair and not try to see the dismissal as a price she had paid for her courage.

Rosa Parks began working at home, taking in assorted sewing jobs. Then another financial blow struck the family. Raymond Parks, who worked at a private barbershop at Maxwell Air Force Base, was told he could not discuss his wife's activism or the bus boycott while he was at work. He became angry and quit his job because he insisted he had the right to mention his own wife on the job. Now the family depended entirely on Rosa Parks's small income.

To make matters worse, the landlord raised their rent by $10 a month, a large increase in those days.

All this turmoil and misfortune caused Raymond Parks to sink into depression. He had always enjoyed drinking gin, but not to extremes. Now he turned to chain-smoking and heavy drinking to relieve his frustration. This added to his wife's distress.

The winter of 1955–1956 in Montgomery was damp and cold. Without full-time employment , Rosa Parks was spending most of her time doing volunteer work for the MIA. She was working harder than ever making sure that boycotting bus riders had a way of getting to work each day. She coordinated shared rides and set up carpools for those who could not walk. Temporary bus stops were set up in black churches so carpoolers had a warm, dry place to wait for their rides.

As the boycott continued, the white business community was suffering. Blacks did not shop in the downtown stores anymore. The bus company, in a desperate attempt to meet expenses, increased fares from ten cents to forty-five cents a ticket. Anger against Rosa Parks and the black ministers was increasing, turning bitter and sometimes violent.

Martin Luther King, Jr., was arrested by Montgomery police on January 26, 1956, for driving thirty miles per hour in a twenty-five-mile zone. He was frisked and put into a squad car. After being fingerprinted and photographed, he was placed in a dirty holding cell. His harsh treatment for a minor traffic violation stemmed from his leadership role in the MIA. Rosa Parks and other black ministers in the MIA were getting death threats on a regular basis.

> The buses stayed empty as the boycott continued.

Parks worried about the effect this was having on her elderly mother and sick husband. She was struggling with doubts over her participation in this effort to overturn segregation when she felt a sudden blessing from God sweep over her. She was praying at St. Paul's AME Church when she felt as if the burdens were lifted from her shoulders. Again and again, throughout this difficult time, Parks called upon her faith. When she had stayed seated on the bus, she said, "I felt the Lord would give me the strength to endure. God did away with all my fear."[9]

On January 30, a bomb exploded at the home of Martin Luther King, Jr. He was away at the time, but his wife and baby daughter were inside the house. King rushed home and discovered that the explosion had blown out all his front windows, leaving a crater on the porch floor. Yet King's family was unhurt, and when an angry crowd of African Americans gathered demanding revenge, King counseled nonviolence and led everyone in singing "Amazing Grace."

The MIA filed a federal lawsuit challenging the constitutionality of the state segregation laws. On February 21,

1956, Rosa Parks and eighty-eight others involved in the bus boycott, including King and twenty other ministers, were indicted for violation of the 1921 Alabama state law barring boycotts.

Rosa Parks was again arrested and fingerprinted, but this time she did not have to go to jail. The mass indictment of all the civil rights activists brought worldwide

In February 1956, Martin Luther King, Jr., Ralph Abernathy, and many others were arrested for the bus boycott.

By her second arrest, Parks was famous,
and news photographers took her picture.

attention to the Montgomery bus boycott. News people from all over the world congregated in the city to watch as the trial of the eighty-eight began on March 19, 1956.

Martin Luther King, Jr., was tried first. He was found guilty and fined $500 or 386 days in jail doing hard labor. He paid the $500 fine and appealed his conviction to a higher court. All the other cases were put on hold as King's case made its way through the federal court system.

On June 5, 1956, a three-judge federal court ruled that

Alabama's bus segregation law violated the equal protection clause of the Fourteenth Amendment to the United States Constitution. The Fourteenth Amendment forbade any law depriving any American citizen of equal protection under the law and full citizenship.

Rosa Parks was gaining nationwide and even worldwide attention now. Eleanor Roosevelt, in her newspaper column, "My Day," praised Parks for her courage. Parks responded to many requests to speak, and she traveled all over the country giving talks about the bus boycott. When she returned home later in June, she found her family had suffered in her absence. Leona Edwards, her mother, was very ill, and Raymond Parks was drinking more heavily than ever.

For the first time in her life as an adult, Rosa Parks was deeply in debt. She could not pay her bills and had to turn to friends for help. Parks had volunteered so many hours for the civil rights cause, and now she was suffering from that sacrifice of time.

Alabama appealed the federal court decision about bus segregation. The final word would come from the U.S. Supreme Court. On November 13, 1956, the Supreme Court upheld the decision, striking down Alabama's segregation laws. The Supreme Court refused to hear additional appeals.

At last, on December 20, 1956, the buses of Montgomery and all other cities in Alabama would be integrated by law.

The thirteen-month-long bus boycott would end. The long and harrowing struggle had resulted in a great victory.

That day, December 20, Rosa Parks boarded an integrated bus without realizing that James Blake was at the wheel. It was an awkward moment as Parks chose a seat. Blake ignored her. When King, Abernathy, and a white minister boarded another bus, the white driver said courteously, "We are glad to have you this morning."[10]

At last, in December 1956, these two African-American men did not have to sit in the back of the bus.

ROSA PARKS

The integration of Montgomery's buses went smoothly for two days, but then pent-up white rage exploded in a series of frightening incidents. On December 23, 1956, a shotgun blast tore a hole in King's front door. Nobody was hurt, but other bombings and shootings were keeping the city nervous. A sniper shot at Rosa Jordan, a black bus rider, shattering her leg. On January 10, 1957, four black churches and the homes of two black ministers were bombed and heavily damaged.

Eventually, calm returned and integration proceeded. On January 30, 1957, police arrested seven KKK members for some of the bombings, but all were acquitted. In April, the city of Montgomery dropped all charges against the eighty-eight activists accused of violating the antiboycott law. Rosa Parks's case was dismissed along with the others.

Montgomery's white community did not find it easy to accept the integrated realities, and bitterness remained. For Rosa Parks, the price her family was paying for being part of the great struggle finally proved too much. It was time to leave Montgomery.

Chapter 7

Civil Rights and Congressman Conyers

n a July night in 1957, Rosa Parks's cousin Thomas Williamson told her to get out of Montgomery, Alabama. "Whitey is going to kill you," he warned.[1] There had been a steady stream of threatening phone calls to the Parks's home from white people who blamed Rosa Parks for playing a major role in dismantling segregation in the state. Raymond Parks had become so depressed by the harassment that he was on the verge of a nervous breakdown. The constant abuse and threats were hard on her aging mother too. There was also another very compelling reason for leaving Montgomery, and that was financial. All during the 382-day bus boycott, Parks made many speeches and appearances, but she never received a speaking fee.

During and after the bus boycott,
Parks became a popular public speaker.

What she was given for travel expenses went to the MIA for taxis and carpools to help the black boycotters go on with their lives.

> It was time for Parks to leave Montgomery.

The Parks family was in serious economic difficulty. Since becoming famous, the woman who would not yield her seat on the bus was virtually unemployable in Alabama. So, although Rosa Parks loved Montgomery and it was painful to move, she decided she must. She sold off the family furniture and packed all her possessions. Parks told the landlord at 634 Cleveland Court that her family would be moving. It was a sad time for Parks. Her husband and mother were in poor health, and the future was uncertain.

Adding to Rosa Parks's gloom was the reaction toward her of many of her old colleagues. The media had built up Parks's image as an icon of the civil rights movement, and some jealousy arose over that. A quiet and humble person, Parks never sought fame or acclaim, but she was getting a lot of attention, and that annoyed some of her fellow civil rights activists. Dr. Ronald Walters, in an article on the life of E. D. Nixon, complained that some people acted as if Parks had "single-handedly kicked off the civil rights movement."[2]

The Parkses headed for the only place where they had family—Detroit. Sylvester McCauley, Rosa's brother, a longtime resident of Detroit, was doing very well. A member of the United Auto Workers, he now worked on the

Chrysler assembly line in the factory where he had once been a janitor.

Sylvester McCauley and his wife, Daisy, owned a roomy home on a large piece of land with a small farm. The family had thirteen children, and even though McCauley made good money at Chrysler, they needed help in feeding all those children. So they raised broccoli, corn, cabbage, carrots, and okra. McCauley also worked in his spare time doing carpentry. When the Parkses arrived, McCauley helped them get a small apartment on Euclid Street.

Rosa Parks enjoyed getting acquainted with all her nieces and nephews. Finally she had the chance to lavish her love for children on some blood relatives. Meanwhile, Raymond Parks started barber school so he could update his skills and qualify for a Michigan barber's license.

Rosa Parks joined the local NAACP and the Urban League. The Urban League was founded in 1910 by blacks and whites to improve housing and employment opportunities for black people in the cities. Parks scrimped and scraped to keep the family going as she looked for work. She never let anything go to waste, making sure she

◆◆◆◆◆◆◆◆◆
Moving North

Two large African-American migrations from the South to the North dramatically changed where blacks lived. The first Great Migration followed World War I, when one million blacks moved north, seeking greater opportunities. Following World War II, two and a half million African Americans left the South for northern cities.

brought unfinished food home on the rare occasions when the family ate out. When Parks made a cup of tea, she always saved the tea bag for a second cup.

Parks had expected to find work in Detroit, but before that happened, she was offered a job in Virginia. At an NAACP function, she met the president of Hampton Institute in Virginia. The Hampton school had been founded right after the Civil War to help former slaves adjust to their new freedom. Now the institute was well known for training black leaders. Parks was offered a job as hostess at the campus's guest residence. The job appealed to Parks because the colder climate of Michigan was harder on her arthritis than Virginia's climate. She hoped to go to Virginia and get settled in her new job, and then find a position for her husband there as well. In the meantime, she worried about leaving her husband and mother in Detroit, but she had no other choice.

Rosa Parks enjoyed working at the Hampton Institute for the year she spent there, but she was unable to find work for her husband. When she returned to Detroit for Christmas in 1958, she found her family suffering greatly. She knew they needed her, so she reluctantly resigned from Hampton and returned to Detroit. She found a job as a seamstress for Leonard and May Stockton's small shop in downtown Detroit. She worked

Parks liked working in Virginia and was sorry to leave her job there.

> Fighting for civil rights did not pay the bills, so Parks had to keep working as a seamstress.

ten hours a day at a sewing machine, making cotton aprons and skirts by the hundreds. She received seventy-five cents for each completed piece, and that motivated her to work even harder to make more money. It was grueling work, but Parks was grateful for the job so she could support her family.

While working at Stockton's Sewing Company in 1961, Rosa Parks met a sixteen-year-old black high school student, Elaine Eason. Elaine was a bright girl who was earning extra money after school for college. When Elaine realized that the woman working beside her on the sewing machines was Rosa Parks—the famous figure of the Montgomery bus boycott—she was astonished. Elaine began asking questions about the movement, about working with Martin Luther King, Jr., and getting arrested. Elaine was not good at the sewing machine, and she lost her job after only five days, but the friendship between the forty-eight-year-old Parks and the teenager grew from that day forward.

Rosa Parks continued her civil rights activism. She had come to see it as her most important role in life. The Southern Christian Leadership Conference (SCLC), an organization coordinating civil rights activism around America, gave Parks honorary membership, and she attended their conventions. Parks also joined in the August

1963 March on Washington for Jobs and Freedom along with Dr. Martin Luther King, Jr., and other activists.

Early in 1964, Rosa Parks learned of a young black man who was trying to get elected to the First District seat from Michigan in the House of Representatives. Thirty-five-year-old John Conyers, Jr., a lawyer and legislative assistant, made his campaign slogan, "Jobs, Justice, Peace."[3] Not yet well known, Conyers was having a hard time getting the attention of the voters.

Rosa Parks decided to join the campaign and help Conyers win votes. Conyers struck Parks as the kind of dedicated, energetic young black politician who would advance the opportunities of African Americans. She phoned Martin Luther King, Jr., and asked him to come

Dr. King's Dream

On August 28, 1963, culminating the March on Washington, Dr. Martin Luther King, Jr., stood on the steps of the Lincoln Memorial. "I have a dream," he told a throng of 250,000 people. His ten-minute oration brought the crowd to cheers, tears, and thunderous applause. King delivered one of the most powerful speeches in American history, concluding with the plea to let freedom ring so that all God's children might at last join hands and sing the words of the old Negro spiritual, "Free at last, free at last; thank God Almighty, we are free at last."

Parks began working for Congressman Conyers.

to Detroit and speak for Conyers. King had made it a rule never to speak in behalf of political candidates. He felt that was not his role, but Parks was very persuasive. She told King that Conyers needed something dramatic to give his campaign a boost. So King came to Detroit and spoke eloquently for the candidate. Conyers won the election by a scant one-hundred-plus votes. Without King's speech, he would have lost. "If it wasn't for Rosa Parks," Conyers later said, "I never would have gotten elected."[4]

As soon as he took office in January 1965, Conyers hired Rosa Parks as a member of the staff in his Michigan office. She went to work on the third floor of the Michigan State Building. Conyers had misgivings when he first hired Parks. "There was some consternation she would be a lightning rod for protest and other civil disobedience," he said.[5] But Parks, finally freed from the sewing machine, turned out to be an excellent choice. All those years working as a volunteer for E. D. Nixon had developed her skills as an organizer, and she was helpful with people. Parks handled the problems of those who lived in Conyers's district, and she arranged the congressman's schedule when he was in Michigan. Parks was the perfect aide—polite, diligent, and dependable.

Still, not all the reactions to Rosa Parks were positive. Some angry letters arrived after she was hired, making demeaning suggestions that rather than working in the congressman's office, she should be cleaning his house or

working in his kitchen. Some of the letters ridiculed Parks. Some went even further. She received rotting watermelons in the mail, alluding to the old stereotypes showing African Americans eating watermelons.

Rosa Parks shrugged off all the unpleasant mail. She had become accustomed to such insults during the Montgomery boycott. She knew there were some people, even in Detroit, Michigan, who were so bigoted that they hated her for what she had done in Montgomery. She never let it get her down.

Chapter 8

"A Sad, Sorrowful Time"

ongressman John Conyers, Jr., has said of Rosa Parks, "She has this gentle sweetness about her."[1] In the office, she was serious and proper, and kind to everyone: a neat, quiet, hardworking person with a deep religious faith. Her personality never changed no matter where she was or what everybody else was doing. But even though she did not join in office parties where liquor was served, neither did she judge other people. "Remember," she said once, "no one is perfect. Keep this in mind as you set examples for others."[2]

Parks was a devoted member of St. Mathews AME Church in Detroit. At first she was the church stewardess, assisting in rituals. Then, after a short time, she was raised to the position of deaconess, which was the highest office a woman could hold in the church. Her duties included promoting the church to the outside world, seeing that sick and needy people in the neighborhood were taken care of, and visiting those in mental hospitals and prisons. Parks threw herself totally into whatever task she was assigned. She wore the uniform of the deaconess, a black bonnet tied under the chin with a white ribbon, and a modest-length dark dress.

Knowing she could often be found at St. Mathews Church, visitors would sometimes stop by just to see her. Many considered her to be the mother of the civil rights movement. To see her taking care of her ordinary duties

Martin Luther King, Jr., right, and his wife, Coretta, helped lead this march through Alabama to demand equal voting rights for African Americans.

in the church seemed amazing. She remained the same humble person as always, even though her name now appeared in newspapers and magazines.

When Rosa Parks heard about someone, she never made up her mind based on the opinions of others. She was especially careful when what she heard was very negative. Such was the case with the Detroit-born Malcolm X, a spokesperson for the Black Nation of Islam. The press described Malcolm X as a proponent of violence and racial hatred, but Parks read all she could about his beliefs. Parks herself worked among the youth of Detroit, many whose lives had been ravaged by drugs and alcohol, so she praised the antialcohol, and antidrug message of the Black Nation of Islam. She favored any effort to rescue black youths from deadly addictions. Parks also said of Malcolm X, "I admired the way he had changed his position from one of distrust toward whites to one of tolerance."[3]

On March 7, 1965, a large, peaceful group of African Americans began to march from Selma, Alabama, to Montgomery to publicize their efforts to get the right to vote. Rosa Parks was home in Detroit when she saw television coverage of the march. City police and Alabama state troopers were attacking the marchers with billy clubs and tear gas. Men and women alike were hurled to the ground. When the marchers took refuge in Brown chapel, the sheriff's posse charged into the church and seized a young man, throwing him through the stained-glass window that depicted Jesus Christ.[4] Rosa Parks was horrified. When Dr. Martin Luther King, Jr., called her to participate in another Selma-to-Montgomery march, she agreed immediately.

Rosa Parks's bank account was almost empty. At her brother's request, his union—the United Auto Workers—paid her expenses to Alabama. The marchers camped on the thirty-eight-acre City of St. Jude, a Catholic charity that served the poor. There, a tent city accommodated the large crowd on the road to Montgomery. This time, Dr. King led the march. Though helicopters roared overhead, and armed troops stood along the route, the people reached Montgomery triumphantly singing, "We *have* overcome."[5] Rosa Parks made no speeches. She was simply one of the marchers, though her presence was noted by reporters.

In April 1965, Rosa Parks became active in the Committee of 1000, a multiracial group working to improve race relations. She also became more deeply involved in women's rights issues. For the first time in her life, Parks publicly showed pride in her African heritage. She made some appearances dressed in colorful African clothing. She shared in the black pride movement, though she continued to reject violence and hatred based on skin color or culture.

During Detroit's 1967 summer race riots, Rosa Parks denounced the violence. After eight days of rioting and vandalism, forty-three people were dead and more than seven hundred were seriously injured. The riots had been triggered by the city's urban-renewal plans, which squeezed out poor black neighborhoods and left hundreds with no place they could afford to live. Among the businesses destroyed by the looters was the barbershop where Raymond Parks worked. He lost all his cutting equipment, and his car was damaged. There was terror and chaos in Detroit, and

Black Pride

In 1917 a black leader named Marcus Garvey came up with a triumphant new cry. He said it was an honor to be black, and that African Americans should be proud.

In those days, toy makers made only white, blue-eyed baby dolls. Garvey demanded black dolls for black children to play with. He raised the cry of black pride, but it did not become widespread until the 1960s, when textbooks finally began to include some of the great African Americans who had been ignored. Storybooks, too, began to show children of color.

Parks said that such actions hurt the cause of civil rights. She decried violence done in the name of black protest.[6]

Rosa Parks and her mother were alone together at home the night of April 4, 1968, when a news bulletin announced the assassination of Dr. Martin Luther King, Jr.

In Memphis, Tennessee, to support garbage workers asking for more just working conditions, King had planned to lead a march the following day. He stepped out onto the balcony of the Lorraine Motel and was chatting with friends below when a deadly shot rang out, taking his life. Parks later recalled that she and her mother "were deeply grieved. We wept in each other's arms."[7]

Parks was so stricken by the news that she decided to go to Memphis to help finish the work that Dr. King had started. When she reached Memphis, she found there was little she could do. Dr. King's funeral was to be held in Atlanta. African-American folksinger Harry Belafonte took Parks there in his private plane. At King's funeral, Parks met briefly with Senator Robert Kennedy, who delivered a moving tribute to King. Only two months later, on June 5, 1968, Robert Kennedy was himself assassinated.

By the 1970s, Rosa Parks had to turn from her civil rights work as her personal problems multiplied. Suffering from stomach ulcers and heart trouble, Parks

Parks was devastated by the news of Dr. King's murder.

Difficult times were ahead for Rosa Parks.

took two bad falls. Once she broke her ankle and another time, her wrist. As she struggled with her health problems, personal tragedy was about to cast a shadow over her family. All three of Rosa Parks's closest family members were gravely ill. She was often frantically shuffling between three different hospitals to visit her husband, her brother, and her mother.

> Personal tragedies in the 1970s cast a dark shadow over Parks and her family.

Raymond Parks had always been a loyal husband. In spite of his weaknesses, Rosa Parks loved her husband dearly. He had accepted his mother-in-law into his home without complaint. Despite his fears about the possible consequences of his wife's activism, he had never demanded that she stop. He respected her right to do what she believed in even when it placed the whole family at risk.

For five years, Raymond Parks had been battling throat cancer, and now the disease was terminal. He died in 1977. His loss had a very profound effect on Rosa Parks. When her husband's stainless-steel casket was placed in the ground at Detroit's Woodlawn Cemetery, Rosa Parks was in deep mourning.

Only three months later, Sylvester McCauley, Rosa's brother, died of stomach cancer. This second serious blow shattered Rosa Parks's life. "Words can't explain the double loss I felt," she said later. "It was a sad, sorrowful time."[8]

Leona McCauley, Rosa's mother, was also ill with cancer. Parks, who was still working full-time for Congressman Conyers, found it difficult to provide care for her ailing mother. She could not afford a live-in nurse, so she placed her mother in a nursing home in downtown Detroit. Parks was so devoted to her mother that she visited her three times a day. That, on top of her heavy work schedule, exhausted her. So Parks rented a new apartment at Bi-Centennial Towers on Alexandria Street, a high-rise building for seniors that charged reduced rent. She brought her mother home and cared for her before and after work, making sure she was comfortable in her absence. "We lived together there until 1979," Parks recalled. Then her mother, ninety-one years old, died. "I found myself all alone," Parks said of the loss.[9]

Sixty-six years old and childless, Rosa Parks was truly alone. Still, she had her work to sustain her, and she had her philosophy of life built on her strong faith. "What really matters is not whether we have problems but how we go through them," she said later. "We must keep on going to make it through whatever we are facing."[10]

In 1979, Rosa Parks was awarded the Spingarn Medal, which is given annually by the NAACP to African Americans who have made significant contributions to the advancement of

> "What really matters is not whether we have problems but how we go through them."

their people. In 1980, she received the Martin Luther King, Jr., Nonviolent Peace Prize awarded by the Fellowship of Reconciliation, a panel of prominent people in Nyack, New York. In 1984, she was honored with the Eleanor Roosevelt Women of Courage Award. Recipients are chosen by the secretary of state, and the prize is given by the president of the United States.

And she kept on going.

Chapter 9

On Her Own

osa Parks had always trusted in the Lord to help her face hardships.[1] After her husband, brother, and mother died, an old friend came to provide support for Parks. Elaine Eason Steele—who had been a teenager when she met Parks in 1961 at Stockton's Sewing Company—was now working with the U.S. district court near Congressman Conyers's office. Rosa Parks and Elaine Steele were always crossing paths as they went about their daily routines. Soon they began commuting to work together, usually in Parks's station wagon.

Elaine Steele had despaired of integration and now favored the formation of a separate black state in the United States where African Americans could flourish in peace. Rosa Parks convinced her to change her position. They began working together on various projects. Parks grew to consider Steele "as close to a daughter as I have had."[2] Under Parks's gentle persuasion, the younger

Rosa Parks celebrated her seventy-fifth birthday in Detroit in 1988.

woman got renewed hope that an integrated society could work for all Americans.

Now in her seventies, Parks suffered with bouts of ulcers and fatigue, and her eyesight was dimming. The time was growing close when she would have to retire from her job and develop new goals and interests.

With Steele's encouragement, Parks took up aerobics, gathered vegetarian recipes, and explored holistic medicine. But the project that really excited her was one she started in 1987 with Steele—the Rosa and Raymond Parks Institute for Self-Development. The goal of the institute was to motivate young people to reach their full potential. The national headquarters was in Detroit's Cadillac Square. Detroit-area students were recruited to travel around the country to visit freedom's landmarks. The trips, called Pathways to Freedom, were designed to give students self-esteem and pride in their heritage. It was hoped that the students would gain an appreciation of the hard work and struggles that brought African Americans to an improved status.

In 1988, Rosa Parks and Elaine Steele led a group of students along the route of the historic march from Selma to Montgomery. Other trips traced the routes of the Underground Railroad. This was a series of safe houses during the era of slavery. Runaway slaves could take refuge at these places as they fled north

> Parks wanted to inspire young African Americans to make the most of their lives.

to freedom in Canada. The students also went to the Great Plains to see where the African-American cavalry, called Buffalo Soldiers, fought on the frontier. They traced the tragic Trail of Tears that drove the Cherokee Indians out of their traditional southern homes into the Great Plains.

Youths from around the country began signing up for the Pathways to Freedom trips. Thousands of young people have taken part in these trips. The institute also developed an intergenerational computer mentoring program, in which young people tutored older members of the community in basic computer skills. In return, the youths had the chance to learn from their elders and gain insight into the past.

In 1988, at the age of seventy-four, Rosa Parks retired from Congressman Conyers's office. She had served there for more than twenty years. Then, in July, Parks attended the 1988 Democratic National Convention in Atlanta, Georgia, where Jesse Jackson introduced her as "the mother of the civil rights movement."[3]

Rosa Parks was very enthusiastic in her work with young people. "It is our job to show them the way," she wrote, "to teach them values, to prepare for the future."[4] Toward this end, Parks wrote three books, all geared toward youths. In 1992, the first of these books was published. Titled *My Story*, Parks told about her part in the Montgomery bus boycott in simple language. The

Rosa Parks is often called the "mother of the civil rights movement."

book was successful, which prompted her to write *Quiet Strength*, also for young readers. The book's content was organized around themes of faith, values, and determination. Parks offered words of encouragement to young people, citing examples of what worked for her.

Over the years, Rosa Parks received many letters from children asking questions about her life and describing their own problems. Parks collected these letters for her third book, *Dear Mrs. Parks*. Included in the book are letters from children and Parks's replies. One boy asked why there was still so much racism in the world, and Parks told him to work for a better world and have faith that it will come. She ended the letter by saying that "we were all created by the same God, who created us all in his image."[5]

A sidelight of Rosa Parks's writing career was that for the first time in her life, she had substantial money to live on. She was never made rich by her books, but she had always worked so hard for her money that the idea of getting checks from the sales of her books was a nice surprise.

It was the 1990s, and Rosa Parks's physical challenges had increased. But she was still active and living her life with the faith and determination she had always showed.

Chapter 10

A Woman of Character

osa Parks had never been outside the United States when, in 1994, she was invited to Japan. Eighty-year-old Parks traveled to Soka University in Tokyo to address the students with the assistance of a translator. She knew that the Japanese students knew who she was, but she had no idea of the kind of reception she would get. Eight thousand Japanese students had lined the streets to greet her, and one thousand sang the civil rights hymn "We Shall Overcome" to her in English. They listened attentively to her message and treated her with the greatest respect.

Back in the United States, Parks continued to be available for personal appearances to help the cause of civil rights. Then, in August 1994, a frightening incident occurred. Parks was getting ready for bed upstairs in her Detroit apartment when she heard a noise downstairs.

> Parks was greeted with great enthusiasm when she visited Japan in 1994.

Parks, who lived alone, heard a thud followed by a male voice. She went slowly downstairs in her bathrobe to investigate. A young black man in his twenties with a pencil-thin moustache stood in the living room. He said that he had witnessed an intruder trying to break in the back door and had stopped the man. Then the man said he thought he should be given a few dollars in return for the service he had rendered.

Rosa Parks told the man she had no money on her, but she would go upstairs to her purse and get him a reward. The man followed Parks upstairs, where his attitude turned hostile. He demanded all the money Parks had. When she hesitated, he began punching her in the face repeatedly. Parks later recalled, "I grabbed his shirt and tried to fight back. I had never been hit like that in my life."[1] The man threw Parks down on the bed, shaking her violently. Parks screamed and pleaded with him to stop hitting her. With blood running from her mouth, she dug in her purse and gave him all the cash in her wallet—$103. Grabbing the money, he ran from the apartment.

Parks called Elaine Steele, who lived across the street. Steele immediately called the police, then hurried over to be with Parks. As the police cars and ambulance pulled up, Parks was grateful not to have been hurt more seriously. "God protected me," she said.[2] She was able to walk to the waiting ambulance in her red bathrobe. By this time, a crowd had gathered. The neighbors shouted, "We love you, Mrs. Parks," as she got into the ambulance. Parks called back cheerfully, "I love you," to the well-wishers.[3]

Parks was treated at the hospital for severe bruises and facial swelling, but she was generally in good condition. When she was released from the hospital the next morning, a news conference had been arranged so she could answer questions about her ordeal. When asked if the attacker knew who she was, Parks said, "He didn't seem to care and I didn't tell him."[4] Later, when recalling the incident, Parks said, "I pray for the young man." She blamed his violent behavior on the conditions under which he was probably raised.[5]

When news of the attack on the gentle, elderly Parks spread, there was widespread indignation. A furious Detroit police chief, Isaiah McKinnon, said, "This is inconceivable. We're talking about a lady who's responsible for changing the course of this country."[6] Detroit police moved quickly to solve the crime. They soon had twenty-eight-year-old Joseph Skippers in custody. In August 1995, about a year after attacking Rosa Parks, Skippers was convicted of assault and sentenced to eight to fifteen years in prison. Skippers blamed his drug addiction for his actions.

> The man who robbed Parks in her home did not know who she was.

The ugly experience did not cause Parks to go into seclusion and avoid contact with people. But she did move to a more secure apartment. She moved to Riverfront Towers, a twenty-four-story apartment building with twenty-four-hour security. From her window high in the building, she was able to see the cruise ships on the Detroit River.

On October 18, 1996, Rosa Parks made a tour of Philadelphia schools, arriving in a white limousine to the

Parks posed in a 1950s bus to commemorate the fortieth anniversary of her famous bus ride.

cheers of "Rosa, Rosa! Rosa!" from the children.[7] This was part of a national tour sponsored in part by the Rosa and Raymond Parks Institute to allow children to see living history. Parks visited Abington Friends School and spoke to fifteen hundred public-school students in the gymnasium of a community college. She told the young people, "You're living in some very perilous times now. . . . That's why I'm here."[9] Parks wore a paisley dress with her hair pulled up in silvery braids. She spoke very softly, but the students listened intently. Commented one student, sixteen-year-old Shawn Jackson, "She's a woman of character." Another excited student said, "This is a lifetime event!"[10] Parks concluded her appearance by telling the cheering students, "Do what you can to make sure that there's freedom and equality and prosperity and peace in the world."[11]

> "We still have a long way to go. . . . I try to keep hope alive."[8]

In 1996, President Bill Clinton awarded Rosa Parks the Medal of Freedom. In 1999, the United States Congress awarded her a Congressional Medal of Honor. During the ceremony, the rotunda of the Capitol was filled with members of Congress, veterans of the civil rights movement, and other dignitaries. Jesse Jackson called Parks "an icon of the country," adding, "Now we know Lady Liberty is real. She is not just a statue," and concluding his remarks saying that "she is a care package, a body of dignity, she is Rosa Parks."[12]

Eighty-six-year-old Rosa Parks was proud to receive the
Congressional Medal, the highest honor given by
the United States Congress.

President Bill Clinton addressed the award ceremony, recalling that he was nine years old in Arkansas when Parks made her stand on that Montgomery bus. He said the story of Rosa Parks should tell everyone that people must never forget the "power of ordinary people to stand in the fire for the cause of human dignity and to touch the hearts of people that have almost turned to stone."[13]

The Southern Christian Leadership Conference now gives the Rosa Parks Freedom Award annually to individuals who have advanced the struggle for human freedom and dignity.

Numerous honorary college degrees and other honors have been bestowed on Rosa Parks. In Montgomery, Alabama, a long street named Rosa L. Parks Boulevard runs through a pleasant, largely black neighborhood. The bus that follows the route bears the destination sign "Rosa Parks."[14]

In December 2000, the Rosa Parks Library and Museum on the grounds of Troy State University in Montgomery, Alabama, was dedicated. Parks attended the ceremony, where three thousand people paid tribute to her contributions to civil rights. The fifty-five-thousand-square-foot building has three floors and is located at the actual place where Rosa Parks was arrested on December 1, 1955.

On that day, eighty-seven-year-old Parks sat in a wheelchair as she was awarded the Governor's Medal of

Honor for Extraordinary Courage. Alabama governor Donald Seigelman gave Parks the medal as a life-size bronze sculpture of Parks was unveiled in the library.

Coretta Scott King, wife of Dr. Martin Luther King, Jr., was present, along with Martin Luther King, III, and Rosa Parks's nieces and nephews. The celebration commemorated the Montgomery bus boycott.[15]

Rosa Parks continues to live her simple lifestyle, reading the King James Bible in large print and praying. Her friend Elaine Steele handles her correspondence and other details because frail health limits Parks's activities.

However, even into her nineties, Rosa Parks was still standing up for her beliefs. In 2003, a movie was made of her life. *Ride to Freedom: The Rosa Parks Story* was nominated for award consideration at the NAACP's annual Image Awards. At the same time, another film, *Barbershop*, starring Cedric the Entertainer, was also nominated for an award. Cedric the Entertainer was chosen as the host for the Image Awards.

Barbershop featured some inappropriate jokes about Rosa Parks and other civil rights leaders. Because Parks regarded these jokes to be demeaning to the civil rights struggle of so many people, she informed the NAACP that she was declining their invitation to attend the Image Awards.

In a letter to the NAACP, Elaine Steele explained, "We with many others do not understand the endorsement the

Parks posed in front of a mural at the Dexter Avenue King Memorial Baptist Church in Montgomery, Alabama.

NAACP gave to the hurtful jokes in the movie *Barbershop* about America's civil rights leaders." Kweisi Mfume, president of the NAACP, regretted Parks's decision not to come to the awards, but he added, "Rosa Parks is a member of our organization, has been long before I was born, and will continue to be."[16]

The Image Awards went on without Parks. *Barbershop* and its star, Cedric the Entertainer, were passed over for any awards, but *Ride to Freedom: The Rosa Parks Story* won for outstanding television movie. Angela Bassett, who portrayed Parks in the film, won for outstanding actress. Rosa Parks thanked the NAACP for "lifting her up."[17]

Morris Dees, founder of the Southern Poverty Law Center in Montgomery, Alabama, said, "When the history of the civil rights movement is written 100 years from now, there are only going to be two significant names— Martin Luther King, Jr., and Rosa Parks. Rosa Parks made a courageous decision and started the civil rights movement. Dr. King took it from there."[18] In describing her legacy, Parks herself put it more simply. "I want to be remembered as a person who stood up to injustice, who wanted a better world for young people."[19]

Chronology

1913—Rosa Louise McCauley is born February 4 in Tuskegee, Alabama.

1924—Becomes a student at Montgomery Industrial School for Girls in Montgomery, Alabama.

1932—Marries Raymond Parks.

1933—Receives high school diploma.

1943—Becomes secretary for Montgomery branch of National Association for the Advancement of Colored People (NAACP).

1955—Attends summer workshop at Highlander Folk School in Tennessee; arrested December 1 in Montgomery, Alabama, for refusing to yield her seat to a white man on the bus; Montgomery bus boycott begins on December 5.

1956—Montgomery bus boycott ends after buses are desegregated.

1957— Moves with family to Detroit, Michigan.

1965—Becomes staff member in Detroit office of Congressman John Conyers, Jr., of Michigan.

1977—Raymond Parks dies.

1979—Receives NAACP's Spingarn Medal.

1980—Receives Martin Luther King, Jr., Nonviolent Peace Prize.

1987—Founds the Rosa and Raymond Parks Institute.

1992—Publishes first book, *Rosa Parks: My Story*.

1994—Publishes second book, *Quiet Strength*; travels to Japan.

1996—Publishes third book, *Dear Mrs. Parks*.

2003—*Ride to Freedom: The Rosa Parks Story* receives NAACP award as outstanding television movie of the year.

Chapter Notes

Chapter 1. The Right to Vote

1. Rosa Parks and Gregory Reed, *Quiet Strength* (Grand Rapids, Mich.: Zondervan Publishing House, 1994), p. 47.

2. Rodney P. Carlisle and Jane Gerhard, "American Politics Southern Style," *American Eras*, Gale Research, 1997–1998. History Resource Center, Farmington Hills, Mich.: Gale Group, Doc. No. BT2301500384.

3. Dennis Ippolito, "Literacy Test," *Dictionary of American History*. History Resource Center, Farmington Hills, Mich.: Gale Group, Doc. No. BT2311023945.

4. Rosa Parks with Jim Haskins, *Rosa Parks: My Story* (New York: Scholastic, 1992), p. 67.

5. Douglas Brinkley, *Rosa Parks* (Thorndike, Me.: Thorndike Press, 2000), p. 95.

6. "Blacks Registered to Vote by Council of Federated Organizations, 1962–1965." *Discovering U.S. History*, Gale Research, 1997. History Resource Center, Farmington Hills, Mich.: Gale Group, Doc. No. BT2104241535.

Chapter 2. Alabama Childhood

1. Rosa Parks and Gregory Reed, *Quiet Strength* (Grand Rapids, Mich.: Zondervan Publishing House, 1994), p. 47.

2. Douglas Brinkley, *Rosa Parks* (Thorndike, Me.: Thorndike Press, 2000), p. 31.

3. Parks and Reed, *Quiet Strength*, p. 48.

4. Ibid.

5. Rosa Parks and Gregory Reed, *Dear Mrs. Parks* (New York: Lee and Low Books, Inc., 1996), p. 80.

6. Janice Min, "Quiet Crusader: Forty Years After She Wouldn't Give Up Her Seat, Rosa Parks Keeps Pushing for Progress," *People Weekly*, December 18, 1995, p. 57.

7. Linda Kulman and David Enrich, "9 Rosa Parks," *U.S. News and World Report*, August 20, 2001, p. 49.

8. Vincent F. A. Golphin, "Taking a Seat for Justice: Living Legend Rosa Parks Reflects on Faith, Dignity and Her Own Courageous Act," *Christianity Today*, April 24, 1995, p. 10.

9. Brinkley, p. 46.

10. Parks and Reed, *Dear Mrs. Parks*, p. 71.

11. Lynda DeWitt, "Rosa Parks, When I Was a Kid," *National Geographic World*, February 1998, p. 19.

12. Ibid.

Chapter 3. Education and Marriage

1. Douglas Brinkley, *Rosa Parks* (Thorndike, Maine: Thorndike Press, 2000), p. 61.

2. Ibid., p. 60.

3. Rosa Parks and Gregory Reed, *Dear Mrs. Parks* (New York: Lee and Low Books, Inc., 1996), p. 54.

4. Brinkley, p. 65.

5. Linda Kulman and David Enrich, "9 Rosa Parks," *U.S. News and World Report*, August 20, 2001, p. 49.

6. Rosa Parks and Gregory Reed, *Quiet Strength* (Grand Rapids, Mich.: Zondervan Publishing House, 1994), p. 46.

7. Ibid.

8. Brinkley, p. 66.

9. "Scottsboro Case," *Britannica Intermediate Encyclopedia*, 12-09-2002. Document page Scottsboro Case.

10. Brinkley, p. 69.

11. Parks and Reed, *Quiet Strength*, p. 46.

Chapter 4. The Strength to Work for Freedom

1. Rosa Parks with Jim Haskins, *Rosa Parks: My Story* (New York: Scholastic, 1992), p. 67.

2. Ibid.

3. Douglas Brinkley, *Rosa Parks* (Thorndike, Me.: Thorndike Press, 2000), p. 103.

4. Ibid., p. 114.

5. Ibid., p. 147.

6. Juan Williams, *Eyes on the Prize: America's Civil Rights Years, 1954-1956* (New York: Viking Penguin, 1988), p. 64.

7. Ibid., p. 65.

Chapter 5. The Arrest

1. Rosa Parks and Gregory Reed, *Quiet Strength* (Grand Rapids, Mich.: Zondervan Publishing House, 1994), p. 50

2. Leslie Anderson Morales, "They've Messed with the Wrong One Now," *Footsteps*, May 2000, p. 10.

3. Ibid.

4. "The Arrest of Rosa Parks, December 1, 1955," *Discovering U.S. History*. Gale Research, 1997, History Resource Center, Farmington Hills, Mich.: Gale Group, Doc. No. BT2104210058.

5. Ibid.

6. Janet Min, "Quiet Crusader," *People Weekly*, December 18, 1995, p. 57.

7. Parks and Reed, *Quiet Strength*, p. 23.

8. Vincent F. A. Golphin, "Taking a Seat for Justice," *Christianity Today*, April 24, 1995, p. 10.

9. Rosa Parks and Gregory Reed, *Dear Mrs. Parks* (New York: Lee and Low Books, Inc., 1996), p. 65.

10. Douglas Brinkley, *Rosa Parks* (Thorndike, Me.: Thorndike Press, 2000), p. 174.

11. Ibid., p. 175.

12. William Roger Witherspoon, *Martin Luther King: To the Mountaintop* (New York: Doubleday, 1985), p. 24.

13. Ibid.

14. Brinkley, p. 178.

15. Leslie Anderson Morales, "They've Messed with the Wrong One Now," *Footsteps*, May 2000, p. 2.

16. Linda Kulman and David Enrich, "9 Rosa Parks," *U.S. News and World Report*, August 20, 2001, p. 49.

Chapter 6. "The Miracle of Montgomery"

1. Douglas Brinkley, *Rosa Parks* (Thorndike, Me.: Thorndike Press, 2000), p. 192.

2. William Roger Witherspoon, *Martin Luther King: To the Mountaintop* (New York: Doubleday, 1985), p. 24.

3. Dianne Swan-Wright, "The Montgomery Bus Boycott," *Footsteps*, May 2000, p. 10.

4. Brinkley, p. 201.

5. Ibid., p. 214.

6. Stephen B. Oates, *Let the Trumpet Sound, A Life of Martin Luther King, Jr.* (New York: Harper, 1982), p. 73.

7. Ibid.

8. Rosa Parks and Gregory Reed, *Quiet Strength* (Grand Rapids, Mich.: Zondervan Publishing House, 1994), pp. 26–27.

9. Ibid., p. 17.

10. Witherspoon, p. 45.

Chapter 7. Civil Rights and Congressman Conyers

1. Douglas Brinkley, *Rosa Parks* (Thorndike, Me.: Thorndike Press, 2000), p. 264.

2. Ronald Walters, "Rosa Parks and E. D. Nixon," *The Black World Today*, June 15, 1999, Article 68652.

3. Brinkley, p. 267.

4. Christine A. Lunardini, "John Conyers, Jr.," *Encyclopedia of African American Culture and History* (New York: Macmillan, 1996) History Resource Center, Farmington Hills, Mich.: Gale Group, Doc. No. BT2312127546.

5. Linda Kulman and David Enrich, "9 Rosa Parks," *U.S. News and World Report*, August 20, 2001, p. 49.

Chapter 8. "A Sad, Sorrowful Time"

1. Linda Kulman, "Rosa Parks, Sat Down and the World Turned Around," *U.S. News.com* special issue, *Crusaders for Justice*, August 20, 2001.

2. Rosa Parks and Gregory Reed, *Dear Mrs. Parks* (New York: Lee and Low Books, Inc., 1996), p. 34.

3. Rosa Parks and Gregory Reed, *Quiet Strength* (Grand Rapids, Mich.: Zondervan Publishing House, 1994), p. 51.

4. Stephen B. Oates, *Let the Trumpet Sound: A Life of Martin Luther King, Jr.* (New York: Harper, 1994), p. 348.

5. Ibid., p. 361.

6. Douglas Brinkley, *Rosa Parks* (Thorndike, Me.: Thorndike Press, 2000), p. 307.

7. Parks and Reed, *Quiet Strength*, p. 39.

8. Brinkley, p. 311.

9. Ibid., p. 317.

10. Parks and Reed, *Quiet Strength*, p. 37.

Chapter 9. On Her Own

1. Rosa Parks and Gregory Reed, *Quiet Strength* (Grand Rapids, Mich.: Zondervan Publishing House, 1994), p. 55.

2. Rosa Parks and Gregory Reed, *Dear Mrs. Parks* (New York: Lee and Low Books, Inc., 1996), p. 23.

3. Sanford Wexler, *An Eyewitness History: The Civil Rights Movement* (New York: Facts on File, 1993), p. 321.

4. Parks and Reed, *Quiet Strength*, p. 81.

5. Parks and Reed, *Dear Mrs. Parks*, p. 83–84.

Chapter 10. A Woman of Character

1. Vincent F. A. Golphin, "Taking a Seat for Justice," *Christianity Today*, April 24, 1995, p. 10.

2. Ibid.

3. "Wounded Angel: Detroit's Fury Is Aroused after Rosa Parks Is Beaten and Robbed," *People Weekly*, Sept. 12, 1994, p. 54.

4. Ibid.

5. Rosa Parks and Gregory Reed, *Quiet Strength* (Grand Rapids, Mich.: Zondervan Publishing House, 1994), p. 37.

6. "Wounded Angel."

CHAPTER NOTES

7. Richard Jones, "Rosa Parks Tells Her Story to Younger Generation," *Knight-Ridder Tribune News Service*, October 18, 1996, p. 1018K2311.

8. Parks and Reed, p. 66.

9. Jones.

10. Ibid.

11. Ibid.

12. Noah Adams, *All Things Considered*, National Public Radio, broadcast June 15, 1999.

13. Ibid.

14. Fred Powledge, *Free at Last: The Civil Rights Movement and the People Who Made It* (Boston: Little, Brown, 1991), pp. 87–88.

15. "Rosa Parks Museum Dedicated," *Jet*, December 18, 2000, p. 8.

16. "Rosa Parks Won't Attend NAACP Awards," Associated Press Online, March 7, 2003.

17. "Barbershop Is Clipped at Image Awards," *Los Angeles Times*, March 10, 2003, p. E-2.

18. Linda Kulman and David Enrich, "9 Rosa Parks," *U.S. News and World Report*, August 20, 2001, p. 49.

19. Parks and Reed, *Quiet Strength*, p. 86.

Further Reading

Brinkley, Douglas. *Rosa Parks*. New York: Viking, 2000.

Celsi, Teresa. *Rosa Parks and the Montgomery Bus Boycott*. Brookfield, Conn.: Millbrook Press, 1991.

Hull, Mary. *Rosa Parks, Young Rebel*. New York: Aladdin Paperback, 2001.

Parks, Rosa, with Jim Haskins. *Rosa Parks: My Story*. New York: Scholastic, 1992.

Parks, Rosa, with Gregory Reed. *Dear Mrs. Parks*. New York: Lee and Low Books, Inc., 1996.

Parks, Rosa, with Gregory Reed. *Quiet Strength*. Grand Rapids, Mich.: Zondervan Publishing House, 1994.

Pinkey, Andrea Davis. *Let It Shine: Stories of Black Women Freedom Fighters*. San Diego: Harcourt, 2000.

Smith, Jessie Carney. *Black Heroes*. Detroit, Mich.: Visible Ink Press, 2001.

Internet Addresses

Rosa Parks biography, interview, and lots of great pictures.
   <http://www.achivement.org/autodoc/page/
   par0pro-1>

Rosa Parks biography with links.
   <http://www.biography.com/search/article.
   jsp?aid=9433715&search=>

The Library of Congress offers an overview of the civil rights era with pictures and illustrations.
   <http://memory.loc.gov/ammem/aaohtml/
   exhibit/aopart9.html>

Index

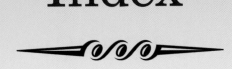

Page numbers for photographs are in **boldface** type.

INDEX